Mark D. Webster

"Yeah Ma, I'm Fine"

Mark D. Webster

Copyright © 2015 Mark D. Webster

All rights reserved.

ISBN: **1511585021**
ISBN-13: **978-1511585026**

DEDICATION

For my Mom and Dad.
Without them, I wouldn't be here.
Thanks for everything.

COVER ARTIST: JUSTIN PIATT

EDITOR: KELSEY FLINT- MARTIN

ACKNOWLEDGMENTS

There are a lot of people I need to thank for their encouragement, support and/or inspiration. First, to my wife, Cindy. Thank you for putting up with my writing when I have other things to do around the house. To my family, and Aunt Bev and Uncle Jerry, you guys are the best. Kelsey, thank you for your help. Justin, once again, thank you for the awesome cover art. Paul Koroluk, for your kind words, and Ron Taffi, AKA Americana Man, you're like a brother. Old friends are the best friends. We may not see each other often, but you're always with me. Dan and Shirley C., my biggest fans. Dean Moriarty for letting me tag along all those years ago. You seriously changed my life. Matt, Woody, The Einstein Brothers, Dave and BJ, and all of the other wonderful people I met during my travels. You created lasting memories for me. And last, but not least, Dora, because I can.

CHAPTER ONE

Looking out the bus window, I was starting to second guess what I was getting myself into. I really wasn't sure, but I needed a change, if only a temporary one. I had been in a relationship with a girl who wasn't eager or willing to break things off. The final clincher for me was when she started sending me letters almost every day. One was even delivered inside a plastic sandwich bag that someone had tied off with a green twist tie because the perfume smelled so bad. Eventually, I quit opening them. A little goes a long way, and a lot goes inside a garbage bag.

To be fair, things had started off well enough between us, but as things often do, they turned sour. At twenty-three, she was four years older than me and was looking to settle down. I was nineteen and just looking to fool around. Eventually, I knew things had to end, so I tried to break it off at first with all the usual stuff. "It's not you, it's me." "You really need someone more mature and closer to your age." It finally became, "Listen, I don't want to see you anymore, now leave."

I was realistic and expected some issues, but I was not prepared for the things that started to happen. Not having a driver's license, I walked everywhere, and my route home was preplanned and predictable. She began randomly following me from work, until one night, she jumped from out from behind bushes and said, "Just thought I'd stop by and say hi!" I have to wonder what she was doing there, especially if I had decided not to go straight home afterward. In retrospect, this behavior isn't as creepy now, but at nineteen, it was unnerving. I began to wonder what more I could do. I finally asked my friends what they would do if they were me. I got advice like, "take her back," "use her and lose her," and "just forget about her." I liked that one best, but she wasn't getting the message.

Finally, I stumbled upon a solution on my own. I was a fan of a rock band called the Doors, and the lead singer, Jim Morrison, mentioned reading *On the Road* by Jack Kerouac in an interview. The premise of the book, a story about cross country hitchhiking and adventures, sounded good, so I went to the local library and checked the book out. I couldn't put it down and I couldn't stop thinking about it afterward. I loved the characters, the storytelling, and the feel of the book. I bought several copies and gave them away, because I was so excited by Kerouac's story. A few friends understood, knowing my free spirit, but many others just didn't get it. It was during my struggles with this girl that I remembered the book, and I settled on the notion of a road trip. I'd go someplace. Maybe even move there, if things panned out. I needed a plan, and then I needed money. Money seems to be a big part of any plan, and this one was no different.

I first decided to tell my folks what I was going to do. Being bit with wanderlust themselves, they were quite supportive if not a little apprehensive, especially my mother.

"How exactly are you going to get where you are going?" my dad asked. "You don't even have a driver's license."

I may not have had a license, but I did have a car. I had bought a 1977 Ford Mustang a while back, making payments weekly from my dad's boss. It was in good condition, and I knew I could get some money for it. The exterior was blue with metal flake and it had a white roof. The hub caps were wire spoke. The interior was clean with white leather seats, and the shift was on the floor. It looked sharp. Even though it had a 130,000 miles and needed a little mechanical repair work, the car ran well. I decided to sell the car and use the money to travel. My dad, being a used car salesman, sold it within two days of putting it up for sale. With my cash problem out of the way, I would soon be on my way.

The next step was to figure exactly how and where I was going. I had no clue. I just wanted to get on the road. I thought I could visit my old friend Ron, the future Americana Man. The Americana Man is a radio personality he would create that now plays some incredible music that most listeners most likely wouldn't hear on top forty or classic rock stations. Ron was living near Seattle, and he told me if I was ever out that way, I could drop in and crash on the couch. We were longtime friends, and he was always true to his word.

How I was going to get anywhere was my final problem. I had done some hitch-hiking, and I didn't mind doing it. Usually it was free, or next to it. Occasionally, someone asked me for a couple of bucks for gas. Still, it was cheaper than a cab and always better than walking in the rain. The bus was another option. The thing with a bus was that you need a destination, which was something I only had a vague idea of.

By chance, my mom happened to see an ad on TV for an Ameripass from Greyhound while I was contemplating this dilemma. An Ameripass was a bus ticket that allowed for unlimited travel for thirty days anywhere in the continental United States. It was the answer to my final problem. I could travel at night, sleeping on the bus, and arrive at a town in the morning. I could explore the place by day and be off to the next town that evening. It was perfect. If I wanted to go someplace the bus didn't, I could hitch-hike. I called the local bus station in Elmira, and they had the tickets. All of my ducks were lined up and ready to go.

So now I had the means to travel, some money, and a destination to start. Beyond that, I decided to just make it up as I went along. The only things I had left were to quit my job, pack some things, and leave. I chose a date about three weeks out. Late spring was on the way, so if I waited a little bit longer, I knew I would have warmer weather on my side. The next day, I went to my boss and told him what I was doing. He laughed and shook his head.

"Good luck with that and be careful," he told me in a thick Italian accent, "and you can come back when you are done."

I thanked him, and we chatted briefly about his

move from Italy to America. It sounded like quite a trip.

That being out of the way, I needed to figure out not only what to pack, but what I was going to pack stuff in. I wanted the freedom to move about, and a large suitcase with all my stuff wasn't going to cut it. I went to the local Woolworth store and poked around. There, I found what I needed: a gym bag. It was large enough to hold what I wanted to bring and it had a shoulder strap and handles. The bag also had a good zipper, which I stood in the aisle testing over and over. I didn't need it breaking while I was gone.

Deciding what to bring was the final step, short of getting on the bus and leaving. I knew I'd need a couple changes of clothes, extra socks, underwear, my toothbrush, and a comb. I crammed all of these things in my bag, along with my camera, and a notebook and pen. I thought maybe I could take notes about where I was going, where I had been, and who I had met. I wanted to bring a few other things, but quickly realized I only had room left for a small hand towel and a washcloth.

The next few weeks went along uneventfully. I discussed my plans with a few friends, but most of them didn't believe I would actually go through with it. Some suggested places to go, others thought I was nuts. I didn't say too much about it to my coworkers; in fact, some didn't know at all. I simply wasn't going to be there anymore, and I couldn't wait to go.

Life proceeded along. The person I didn't mention it to, and I made my friends swear not to mention it either, was the ex-girlfriend. She had been trying harder as of late to convince me that we should try to "work this thing out." I, on the other hand, wanted to end this thing…yesterday or sooner.

About a week before I left, I was done working. They held paychecks back a week, so I had one last paycheck to go with the cash I had saved, as well as the money from selling my car. I wasn't rich, but I felt like it. I also started feeling sick. Suddenly, and for no comprehensible reason, I began having diarrhea and vomiting. For that entire final weekend, I was ill.

"Maybe you better stay home," my dad told me.

"It must have been something I ate," I reasoned.

My mom suggested another possibility. "Maybe it's just nerves. It'll go away."

It did go away and by that Monday I was fine. Tired, but fine.

That morning, my dad and I went to the bus station in Elmira. It was behind a little bar and restaurant. The bus station was painted black for some reason, and was kind of a gloomy place. The ticketing agent stood out for being nice though.

"Where you going?" she asked.

"I don't really know."

"That could be a problem in buying a ticket. I need to know where you're going, before I can sell you a ticket to get there."

"It's not that simple. I want to travel until I find a place."

She looked at me like I was insane. I needed to explain what I was doing and quickly. My father stood there, not saying a word.

"Ma'am, I saw an ad on TV for something called an Ameripass. I called here a few weeks ago and asked about them. Do you still sell them?"

"Yes."

"Can I buy one?"

"Yes, but you still need to be going someplace."

She then explained to me how it worked: thirty days, unlimited bus riding, but to and from *someplace*. I needed a someplace to travel to. I knew that, at some point, I wanted to drop in on Ron near the city of Seattle, Washington. So I decided that's where I would go first.

"Okay, how about Seattle, Washington?"

"Which route do you want to take? Most direct or scenic?" she asked me.

"I don't care."

"Me either," she said dryly. "I'm not the one taking this trip."

"I haven't been a lot of places. Could you just pick a route?"

She must have felt bad for me, or maybe she just wanted me to leave, because she reached under the counter and pulled out a map of the United States. With a yellow highlighter, she traced out a route on the map to Seattle.

"Half-scenic, half direct. That'll get you there,

but you'll have to figure out what else you are doing once you get there."

Her markings went through Cleveland, Chicago, and Omaha, to name a few of the cities I actually recognized.

"That'll work. Thanks for your help. I appreciate it."

"You're welcome. I was young once."

She rang everything up, and I gave her my money. It left me about twenty-five dollars in my wallet. It was a sum my dad couldn't help but notice.

"Is that all the money that you have left? You can't live on that."

"Dad, relax. I kept some cash in my wallet, some in my bag's inside lining, some in the pocket of my jeans, and some under the insoles of my sneakers. I didn't want it all in one place in case I lost my wallet."

"Okay, just checking. You can't blame me for worrying."

"I know. I've got it all under control."

The truth was that it wasn't under control at all.

I just wanted to go. I was still that little kid inside, walking around the corner of the block just to see what was there.

The bus wouldn't leave for a couple of hours, and my dad had to get back to work. He asked me again if I was going to be all right. I assured him I was and we said our goodbyes. He then headed out of the bus station, and I plunked my butt in a seat to wait. I had never ridden a bus before, with the exception of a yellow school bus when I was younger. That was about to change in a big way.

Finally, the bus arrived and pulled into a parking place. I watched several people get out and be greeted by friends or loved ones. The driver opened the side door on the bus and removed some luggage. I had wondered where they stored stuff. After they were done, he began accepting passengers. I got on, and as I sat next to the window, I gazed out and wondered what I was getting myself into. Everything was quiet. There weren't many people getting on the bus. Then suddenly, the engine came to life and shook me out of my thoughts. The driver walked the length of the bus and checked tickets. He then went to his seat and started the engine. The bus rumbled into motion. Backwards at first, the bus driver skillfully maneuvered the bus into position, and proceeded to lurch forward, directing us into traffic, through the city and onto the highway. I wasn't familiar with Elmira, so I looked around curiously as we traveled through the city. It seemed like a distant world, although it was only twenty miles or so away from my home. I would soon realize that it was much more like home then some of the places I was about to go. This country we live in was, and is, more vast and diverse than described in any news program, movie, or history book.

CHAPTER TWO

Looking out the window, I began thinking I should be writing all the details down: what things looked like, what time I traveled here or there, and other things like that. With good intentions, I started a journal.

"Day one: Went to Elmira, bought ticket, got on the bus"

It wasn't much of a start, but it was something. I looked through my papers and discovered that the first stop was going to be in Buffalo, NY, and then I would be on to Cleveland. I had never been to either place, so this seemed exciting.

"Day one: Going to Buffalo, then Cleveland, Ohio."

I was going to have to find a way to make these journal entries more interesting. What did I know about either place? Buffalo was the home to the Buffalo Bills football team and the burial place of President Millard Fillmore. It was also home to my favorite hockey team, the Buffalo Sabres. Cleveland was home to the Indians baseball team, and the Browns football team. Other than that, my only notion of Cleveland was what Howard the Duck said: "The land of Cleves." So I really didn't have much to go on, but thought I should try again.

"Day one: Going to Buffalo, the home of the greatest sports franchises of all time, the Buffalo Bills and the Buffalo Sabres. Also the burial place of one of the most beloved and respected presidents ever, President Millard Fillmore."

Not bad, except I wasn't trying to write fiction or a tourist brochure for the local chamber of commerce. I ripped the page out of my notebook and crumpled it up. I then realized I had no place to throw it, so I stuffed it in my bag. I decided then that writing about an adventure would have to wait for the adventure to actually happen. Truth in fiction is good, not so much the other way around.

After a few hours, the bus arrived in Buffalo, and it was just starting to get dark. Buffalo is a blue collar town, made tough from cold, snowy winters and has been made tougher by the recent rough economy. The setting sun outlined the skyline and the outline of the buildings fascinated me. It was my first view of a big city. The bus station was located in the city and was part of a complex. The driver announced that this was only a fifteen minute stop and that he would be leaving on time, so if anybody was getting out to go to the bathroom or to eat, they had better get right back because he wasn't waiting… message understood. He didn't seem terribly friendly or patient, but at least a person knew where he stood with him. I didn't have to go to the restroom, and I wasn't hungry, so I opted to remain on the bus. Several others got off and a few new people got on. No one sat next to me, so I waded up my duffle bag as a pillow against the window and tried to sleep

Sleeping on the bus is an art form of desperation. You have to be completely exhausted to do it. As the bus fills with people, or starts and stops, sleep is interrupted. So far no one had sat by me, so I didn't have any of the nightmare stories you hear about rude or bizarre seatmates. It was, to be honest, a very uneventful adventure so far. I was on a ride less interesting than going to elementary school when I was a kid. Riding the bus back then was an adventure every day. Some days it was trying to find a seat, and other days it was trying not to get noticed by the bully. One day, a bus driver got so upset at the antics of one of the kids that he did something a bus driver couldn't get away with today. He pulled the bus over and left the kid on the side of the road, standing there with his lunch pail and books. It was a very different world back then.

Arriving in Cleveland in the dark was, if possible, less interesting than I could have ever imagined. I grabbed my bag, made sure it was zipped close, and headed off the bus. I didn't have to change buses until I got to Chicago, but I was getting hungry, I needed to use the restroom, and I wanted to stretch my legs. There was a sandwich shop nearby, and I bought a plain hamburger and a coffee. They were the cheapest things on the menu. I ate my dinner, did my business, and headed back to the bus. I wasn't the first one on this time, and before I managed to get on, a line had quickly developed behind me. Apparently, there weren't a lot of people going to Cleveland, but there sure were a lot leaving. I walked toward the back of the bus and found a seat next to the window. As I sat there, I watched more and more people get in line to get on the bus. I knew someone would be sitting next to me. I was hoping for an attractive woman, with whom I could have an interesting, stimulating conversation or, if I couldn't, at least she would be pleasant to look at. But, being more realistic, I figured it would be someone with a crying baby and an attitude that would drive me crazy.

It turned out to be neither. As I was looking out of the bus window, I heard a voice ask, "Is anyone sitting here?"

I looked up to see a young guy, about my age, looking down at me.

"Nah, it's all yours."

"Thanks, man. My name is Matt. What's yours?"

I introduced myself, and Matt sat down.

"Where are you headed?" he asked me.

"Right now I'm going towards Seattle to visit a friend. He doesn't know I'm coming though. After that, I really don't know yet. How about you?"

"I'm going to San Diego, California to stay with my sister and her husband. My mom thinks it would be better there than here. My neighborhood is getting a little rough to be in."

"What's going on there?"

"Gangs, drugs, stuff like that. My mom was worried I might get caught up in it or something. I told her I'd be fine, but she didn't believe me, I guess."

"That's a lot different than where I'm from."

"Where are you from?"

"Well, originally Herkimer, NY, but currently Corning, NY. Corning is a nice little town and compared to where you're from, it would be extremely dull. People with kids like it because it's safe. Old people like it for that reason too, I guess."

"Where's that other town you mentioned?"

"Herkimer? That's upstate NY. People hear New York and they only think of New York City. That's really a small part of the state though. Truthfully, the parts of the state that I've lived in are mostly old farms and old friends. Corning has a glass factory, so it's called a city but it's more like a small town. My folks left Herkimer when my dad got a job offer in Corning. He's a car salesman. We've been there ever since."

"Miss it?"

"I miss some of my friends there. The town

itself is changing, a little good, a little bad. You don't see things change as much when you're in the middle of them, but sometimes when you step away, it's much more obvious."

"Which town do you like better?"

"They're both different. Corning is actually pretty nice, and there's more to do. I think there's a lot more money there. Herkimer's pretty small, and it doesn't have the industry, but it's a nice area. I guess I like them both. What does your family do?"

"My mom stayed home raising kids, and I'm the last one. My sister lives in California. She's a teacher. My mom's proud of her. I just graduated, and my mom wants me to live with my sister, so I can go to college and become something."

"Like what kind of something?"

"I don't know. Something smart that makes a lot of money, I guess."

"Is your mom moving out there too?" I asked.

"No, she says she's too old to move out there, but she might come for a visit."

"I guess that would be okay."

After that exchange, the two of us sat quietly back in the seats for quite a while. I gazed out the window. It was funny to me how much upstate New York and Ohio looked alike. I didn't know what I expected, perhaps huge differences.

The bus drove on into Cincinnati. Once again, a few people got on and a few got off. As we rode through the city, I couldn't help but sing the theme to the television show *WKRP in Cincinnati*. It had been one of my favorite shows, but it ultimately got lost in shuffling timeslots, so I never knew when it was going to be on.

We arrived in Chicago, Illinois just before lunch. Coming into Chicago, the first thing you see is the skyline. Large, imposing building were surrounded by clouds, which, to me, looked like an arm with a muscle flexing. On the shoulder of that arm was most likely a chip, so the city could dare anyone to try and knock it off. Cities, I would later learn, have their own personalities. Chicago looked resilient, and it was. The winters, the people, and the rigors of life have made Chicago a rugged, blue collar city, strong and tough.

The bus station in Chicago leads out to the street. I had asked Matt if he wanted to go look around a bit before the next bus left. Chicago was where we would part company and we each had a different bus to catch. He was headed toward California, and I was going to Omaha, Nebraska. The Greyhound Bus sign outside was huge and easy to see, even though the weather was cool, overcast and lightly raining. We looked up at the Sears tower and I knew it was tall without really being able to see that far up. It's neck-wrenching to look at just part of it up close. I took a few pictures with the disposable camera I brought along and knew I looked like a tourist.

"Mark, I've got to get back to the bus station," Matt announced, after looking at his watch. "Besides, I'm getting a little hungry. There's a Burger King inside. What do you say to lunch?"

Downtown Chicago, Illinois

"Sounds like a plan to me. Let's head back."

We walked back to the bus station and I was glad to get out of the rain. It hadn't been a hard rain, more like a sprinkle, but it made me feel damp. We ordered our food and, like in Cleveland, I ordered a coffee and a burger. I also ordered fries as a bonus on account of Matt and me parting company. That, and I was hungry.

We sat in the booth facing each other and talking, when two young guys came in and sat next to us, one on each side of the booth.

"May we join you guys?" one of them asked.

"Looks like you already have," Matt answered, looking at them.

Both of them appeared to be in their early twenties. They were tall, about six foot five or so. They were both surprisingly well dressed. High end dress shoes, khaki pants, dress shirts, gold watches and chains. One had a black dress leather jacket, and the other wore one in red. They both looked like slick hustlers and bad news.

The one in the red jacket spoke next. "Do you guys have any extra money? You see, my friend and I are hungry. You guys have lunch and we need it. We're starving."

Matt looked at him. "No man, I had just enough for mine and that was it. Nothing extra."

They looked at me.

"Sorry, I just spent what I had, too."

The two of them looked at the two of us, making me very uncomfortable. The guy in the black jacket rubbed his face a little, and changed the tone in his voice. He was now more to the point.

"I don't think you understand. You see, we're hungry. We ain't got any money, and we need to eat. Now you aren't going to deny some brothers some food are you? Something as basic as that, are you? Are you listening to me?"

The other guy spoke, "You don't need a little help finding it, do you? We can be very helpful guys. It's just the way we are."

Matt looked at me and then looked at these two guys. He then proceeded to reach inside his coat. He took out a small book. I looked at him and wondered what he was up to. I didn't have to wonder long.

"Brothers, I have something here for you better than a burger. More filling than french fries. It's something that will stay with you longer than money. It's God's word, and he has a plan for you right here in this Bible."

The two guys looked at Matt in surprise and then looked at me. I'm sure I looked as surprised as they did. Matt then proceeded to climb onto the bench of the booth, standing up to address the restaurant.

"Now if you'll listen to what I have to say, God can save you now from whatever hungers you," he said, raising his voice.

"What are you doing? Sit down," one of the guys said.

"We don't need any of that," said the other.

Matt was on a roll, but I didn't know what to think or where this was going. He seemed to have a plan, though.

"What you need is Jesus. Pray with me now."

Right about then, the other people in the restaurant couldn't help but notice Matt, and I began to realize that was his intention. The guys who joined us noticed everyone watching.

"Brothers, confess to God above and come to church with me," Matt said, his voice rising like he was preaching a Sunday sermon and his arms waving in the air.

Our two visitors again looked back and forth between Matt and I.

"Your friend isn't right," the one guy said to me.

"We got to be leaving," the other said to both of us.

"You should be leaving right now and get to church to see the Lord. He is waiting for you both," Matt announced to them, never missing a beat.

By this point, the two of them had stood up and were making their way out of the building's main door. They turned and headed up the street, obviously unnerved by what had just happened and wanting no part of Matt and his Sunday sermon.

"What was that and where did it come from?" I asked, still trying to take it in.

Matt looked at me and started laughing. "My old pastor told me to do that if I ever ran into trouble on my way to see my sister. I just pretended to be him. I'll have to tell him it worked out pretty good."

"Do you always carry a Bible around?"

"Nah. My mom made me bring it. It's just a little New Testament. I think it's a Gideon Bible. You should get one."

"That's a good idea. I'll have to try and remember that."

I shook my head and laughed some more at what just happened as I started to eat again. Somehow, while all this was happening, my coffee and fries managed to get colder than room temperature. Cold fries are gross, but I was hungry and finished them anyway. Matt finished his lunch, too, and then he reached into his bag for something.

"Want some cookies? My mom made them."

"Sure, thanks," I said, taking the few that he handed me. They were incredible chocolate chip cookies, still soft and loaded with chocolate.

"These are great, Matt. I don't know if I would have shared them if they were mine."

"I've got a whole bagful and my mother promised to mail me some more later."

"Moms can be awesome. Thanks again."

Matt looked at his watch and stood up. "Hey, I've got to go. Good luck with your trip and wherever it is you're going."

"Yeah, you too. I hope you like California."

"I'm sure I will. See you."

"See you."

We shook hands and he headed toward his bus.

I watched him walk away and then I headed toward the restroom. My own bus was departing soon, and I wanted to wash up a little. I was sure I needed to clean up and there was no place on the bus to do it. I went to the sink, opened my bag, and took out my washcloth. The faucets were still the type with both hot and cold knobs, but only the cold would turn on. I washed up quick, and put the wet washcloth in the plastic bag I had brought with me. The soap in the dispenser had been the generic pink liquid, and it worked okay for cleaning, but now I smelled like bathroom soap. I supposed it was better than body odor.

I dried off using paper towels and stuck a few in my bag in case I needed to blow my nose. Turns out, I had forgotten to pack some Kleenex. I gathered my stuff and headed for the bus. The driver in the Chicago station checked your ticket before you got on. No ticket, no bus ride. I found a seat next to a window and looked outside, watching people. I couldn't help but notice that the two guys who hassled us during lunch were still milling around the station. I figured they were still looking for someone to hustle. Maybe they really were hungry, but I was glad they were outside and not in the bus. I turned my attention to the inside of the bus to see if there was anyone who looked interesting. Everyone looked pretty normal and there weren't any people to talk to, but at least I finally had something to write about. I finally had some adventure. It wasn't like anything I would have ever planned, but maybe adventure never is. I took out my notebook and jotted down a few things. So far, this was turning out to be pretty cool.

Mark D. Webster

CHAPTER THREE

As the bus pulled away from the station and started to work its way through the city, I stared out the window and watched as we passed by the buildings, the traffic, and the people. I was glad I didn't live there. My last experience aside, this city was too big and too busy. The old saying, "it's a nice place to visit, but I wouldn't want to live there," was holding true. I was quickly realizing that I was more small town that I had imagined. I always knew that there was nothing wrong with being from a small town. Each small town has a special comfort and glory all their own. For the first time, I was learning to appreciate that.

After a few stops, more people getting on the bus were closer to my age, and they seemed interested in talking to one another. I was thankful for this, because I was dying for some conversation. The first guy to get on was a tall, thin man about twenty-two or twenty-three. He wore a cowboy hat, a denim jacket, blue jeans, and sneakers. Most of his clothes were well-worn, but not tattered, and his sneakers were brand new. They were white and stood out against the rest of him. He was lanky, but looked comfortable, and spoke with a southern accent. He announced to everyone on the bus that he was going to be working on his aunt and uncle's ranch for the summer. He sat down in front of me and immediately reclined.

Before the bus had even moved, he hollered out and laughed, "Can't wait to get there. Are we there yet?"

Then, the bus jarred and rolled onward. I was starting to worry that this would be a long trip, with Tex upfront chattering to no one in particular. I didn't hear him offer up his name, but he looked like someone named Tex.

Soon the bus stopped again, and a young girl, maybe eighteen or so, got on the bus. She was petite and had long brown hair that hung loosely over her shoulders. Wearing almost no makeup, she glowed with a natural beauty that contrasted that shadows and drab of the bus. She didn't go unnoticed by the cowboy either, especially when she sat in the seat directly across from him.

"Hi. Where you heading to?" he asked her.

"Uh…" she paused, not sure if she should tell him. " I'm going to my Dad's house in-"

Cutting her off mid-sentence, Tex talked over her. "I'm going to my aunt and uncle's ranch. They hired me for the summer. I'll be runnin' the place for them before you know it. They've got cattle and I know all about that. I've been around cattle all my life."

She gave him a strange look.

"I was raised on a farm," he continued. "I'm going to make enough to buy my dad's old truck, and then it'll be mine."

"Really?" she answered with mock enthusiasm.

"Yep. Then I can make some extra money hauling and stuff like that. What are you going to do at your dad's house?"

"Visiting, that's all."

"That's good. It's good to visit."

The conversation went back and forth like that for quite a while. She would get out one sentence and then he would jump in for another five minutes. Eventually, I tuned them out and dozed with my head against the window.

At the next stop, no one got on and no one got off. It was only significant because the bus driver announced, in a static-filled monotone, that we would be switching buses at the next station in an hour or so. We should be expecting an hour long wait, so it would be a good time to go eat and whatever we needed to do, but we could not remain on the bus.

We reached the stop to change buses in what was basically the middle of nowhere. I thought it was a strange place to swap buses, but while I was waiting, I found out that the bus was starting to have some sort of mechanical issues. They wanted the driver to get the bus to the closest stop on route to switch things around. Everything went smoothly, and interestingly enough, just about everyone returned to the seat where they were on the first bus.

At the next station, three more folks got on the bus. First on was a guy in his mid-twenties. He was short, somewhat toned, and, as I would find out later, from France. He made a beeline for the pretty girl sitting across from Tex.

"Are you sure she wants you sitting there?" Tex asked him.

"I'm sure she would tell me if she had any

objections," the Frenchman replied.

"If he gives you any trouble, you let me know. We know how to deal with guys like him where I come from."

The young girl looked up, half smiling, half worried, and totally flattered.

"No, he's fine. He can sit here. I don't mind."

"Thank you, mademoiselle," the Frenchman said as he sat next to her.

Tex sulked back into his seat. I watched as another person joined our section of the bus. The raw-bone, rugged-looking character sat next to Tex. The seat strained as he threw himself into it. Wearing a leather jacket, jeans, and motorcycle boots, he looked mean. He has a buzz cut and his face had slightly more stubble on it.

"I'm sitting here, okay?" he told Tex.

Tex just looked at him and nodded quietly, still sulking. In fact, it was the quietest I had heard him so far.

The third person to get on the bus was a cowboy, about thirty years old. He walked with a slight limp and looked like he was in pain. He was dressed in well-worn and faded blue jeans. He had on brown cowboy boots, a plain white long sleeve dress shirt, with a white t-shirt visible underneath. His belt buckle was oversized and made of silver and gold with a bronco on it. I couldn't quite read the lettering on it.

"Is anyone sitting here sir?" he asked me.

"No, feel free," I replied, studying him.

"Thanks, man," he said, offering his hand. "My name's Woody. What's yours?"

"Mark."

"Well, Mark, where you from?" he asked.

"I'm from Corning, New York. I'm just sorta out exploring the country. How about you?"

"You a cop, or a support agent, or anything like that?"

I shook my head no.

"I'm from Oklahoma. A little town you ain't never heard of. I'm lookin' for a place where I can do some logging, a place where they don't ask too many questions about you or where you're from. You see,

I've got a couple of ex-wives who'd like a whole lot of back payment I don't intend on paying any time too soon. The judge saw things differently than I did and was about to throw me in jail. The way I figured it, I could go out West someplace and work to earn some money, and maybe, if I make enough, I can send them enough to keep the judge happy. I sure wasn't going to make anything sitting in County."

"I see," I answered, not really knowing what to say.

"I used to ride rodeo. That's where I won this belt. Now my back hurts, and my leg ain't quite right anymore."

"So you're going to do logging?"

"Mark, a man can only do what he knows. I like being outdoors - ranching, logging, even construction. It would kill me having a desk job, just being inside all the time. What do you do?"

"I worked in a little bakery."

"Did you like it?"

"Well enough, I guess."

"You're young still. You'll get it figured out.

Where did you say you were headed off to?"

"Right now I'm headed to Seattle, Washington to pop in on a friend of mine. From there, I don't really know."

"I'll ride with you that far. I like you. We can watch each other's backs. What do you say?"

"Sounds good."

"It's settled then," he said to me, reaching out his hand.

I shook his hand, and now I had another traveling companion. Woody turned out to be pretty interesting to speak with, especially as the hours went by. He told me about his life riding in the rodeo. Everything about him seemed like it was taken from a country song. He made enough money on the rodeo circuit to usually go on to the next place. Women were primarily a means to an end and a source of a one night companionship while he healed up his wounds and cured his boredom. Friends were few, but solid in his mind, and once he decided that you were a friend, there wasn't any other way to it.

I dozed off for a bit while he was talking. It

wasn't that his stories weren't interesting, but his ability to talk far outlasted my ability to listen. Several folks got on and off at the various stops, but the core group stayed on.

I woke up to Woody poking me in the ribs. "What?" I asked, a little irritated at the intrusion of my sleep.

"You've got to listen to these to chuckleheads in the seats ahead of us"

"What? Who?" I asked again.

"The two guys in the seats ahead of us. Just listen."

I sat there trying to clear my head and wake up. It seemed that Tex and his seatmate were having a rather heated debate on the best place to build a house.

"I'm telling you, you don't have a clue what you're talking about. The best place to build a house is on top of a hill," Tex declared.

"You have no idea what you're talking about," the other guy countered. "Flat land is where you should build it. Everything's already level. All you gotta do is go up. If you live on a hill, the house won't be level and you'd have to pump the water up to the house. It's a lot more work for everything and everybody. You're constantly going up the hill or down the hill. It's up or down."

Tex stared at him, not about to let this guy get the better of him.

"Why do you think rich people live on hill tops?"

"So they can look down on everybody."

"Very funny. That's not it at all. They do it on account of the mud slides," Tex told him matter-of-factly.

"Mud slides? You're kidding me, right? You've been out in the sun too long without your hat. Did you think that up on your own or did you get some help?"

"I'm telling you, it's because of the mudslides."

"Okay, tell me what on earth the mudslides have to do with it."

Woody turned and looked at me. "This oughtta be real good. These two have going back and forth for hours. There's not a bit of common sense between them."

Tex took a breath. "When you build a house, you have to think about where it's going."

"Where's it going?" the other guy interrupted.

"Just listen, will you? Let me talk, so I can explain it to you. When you build a house along a river, you have to know where it's going to go if there's a flood. You don't want it going over a waterfall or anything like that, do you? Of course not."

I just looked at Woody, not believing what I was hearing.

"So if you build a house, you're going to want to build it someplace safe and secure. What's safer than the top of a mountain?"

"So what if there's a mudslide?"

"That's why you build your house at the top of the mountain. If your house is at the top and there's a mudslide, your house will slide safely down the hill, while all the other houses are getting crushed by the mud."

Tex then stood up and turned to face Woody and me.

"You guys understood all that, didn't you? I

don't understand his problem."

"I heard every word," I replied, repressing a smirk.

"You see? They know I'm right," he said, reseating himself. "My house would be safe and yours, my friend, would be gone."

Woody turned to me, speaking softly, "I knew this was going to be good."

Tex turned and looked out the window, his arms crossed and giving off the impression of someone quite satisfied with himself. It was a rare moment of silence for him. Across the aisle, the Frenchman was still busy chatting up his seatmate. His accent reminded me of the Inspector from the *Pink Panther* films, and she seemed to be enjoying his attention. Woody closed his eyes and started dozing. I looked out the window and wondered what was going to happen next. Omaha, Nebraska was our next stop and while I didn't know much about it, we were going to be there for a long stop over and I was going to learn

CHAPTER 4

We arrived in Omaha early in the evening. The bus pulled into the station and shuddered to a stop. The driver thanked everyone for traveling with him and explained that this bus would not be traveling any farther, so everyone would have to transfer to another bus. Through some conversation, and a little bit of eavesdropping, I was able to figure out that everyone in our small group would be going to Salt Lake City, Utah before dispersing to parts unknown. Everyone got out of the bus, and we stood there staring at each other and at our luggage.

"Is that all you're carrying?" the girl asked me, noticing my duffel bag.

"Yeah, I travel light," I replied.

"What do you say we get something to eat?" asked Tex.

"What's everyone want?" I asked.

"There's a Domino's Pizza place right over there," Woody spoke up. "We could all pitch in a few bucks and split a pizza or two."

Everyone agreed, and I was nominated to get the pizzas. I walked down the street to the Domino's. It was a thin building with only one doorway. The door was absurdly heavy and difficult to open.

"You don't want anyone dashing out of here, do you?" I asked, looking at the man making pizzas behind the counter.

"That's never a problem. What can I get for you tonight?"

"I need to order a couple of pizzas with extra cheese to go."

"That's the only way we sell them here," he answered.

"With extra cheese?"

"No, to go. There aren't any tables or chairs."

"Got it."

He rang me up for the pizzas and told me to be sure to leave a tip in the tip jar for the extra cheese. I looked at him for a second, and then placed a few dollars in the tip jar.

"Thank you, sir."

"You're welcome," I answered, puzzled by the whole idea of tipping for a pick-up order.

I stood there looking out the window and watching the traffic. After a short wait, the pizzas were ready. I took them and walked over to where I had left everyone standing. Noticeably, Tex was nowhere in sight.

"Aren't we missing someone?" I asked, presenting the pizzas.

"Oh, he went to get a drink. He'll be right back," the Frenchman responded.

"Mark, how much cheese did you order on this pizza?" Woody asked me, opening the box.

"Just extra, like we all agreed. Did he rip us off?"

"There's as much cheese as there is crust," he said, laughing. "I won't be able to shit for a week."

I then realized what the pizza guy meant by tipping for extra cheese.

"I'll be glad when Tex gets back here with something to drink," I said to Woody.

About that time, Tex came strolling in with a bag in his hand. I thought he must have bought a two liter of soda.

"They didn't have my usual stuff, so I bought a bottle of vodka instead," he said, offering up the bottle. "Who's first?"

"Just a thought here, cowboy," Woody said, "but you might want to slide that bottle back in the bag, at least in public. Let's go to the park over there, where we can at least sit and eat."

"That's a good idea," I chimed in, thinking that smoothing everything over would be the best way to go. And besides, I wanted to eat some pizza.

We wandered over to one of the tables that had benches in the park and I set the pizzas down. As soon as the boxes were opened, everyone grabbed some pizza and started eating. The vodka bottle was passed around and Woody took a long drink. I was impressed – there were probably two or three shots in that swallow.

"Here you go, Mark. Take a mouthful to wash that cheese down," he said as he offered me the bottle. I took the bottle a little reluctantly, but I wasn't about to turn down a drink. I carefully brought the bottle to my lips and took a drink. Wrinkling my face, I swallowed. I knew I didn't look as composed as Woody.

"What did you think?" Woody asked.

"Smooth," I lied, with a rasp in my voice that wasn't there before.

"Smooth? Hell, it didn't taste any better than paint thinner, and it would probably do a better job."

"You're right. It's a little rough," I confessed.

Everyone laughed, proceeding to eat pizza and pass the bottle. I was starting to feel the vodka a little more with each swallow.

"Hey, why don't we play on the playground?" the girl suggested, running toward the playground equipment.

The Frenchman followed, as did both the Einstein cowboy and biker guy from the seats in front of me. I looked at Woody, as if waiting for approval. He looked at me and motioned for me to join the rest of the group.

"I'm going back to the bus station. I've had

enough of the finest wine Boise ever made," he said as he stood up.

I watched him limp his way toward the bus station, dragging his logging equipment with him. Then, I jogged over to the playground to catch up with the others. There were swing sets, slides, and a merry-go-round that you push around and jump onto. The girl went for the swing set and the Frenchman positioned himself behind in order to "help" push. Tex went for the slide, going up the ladder with no hands and standing at the top like a school boy trying to get the prettiest girl's attention. I laid on the merry-go-round looking up at the night sky. After a few minutes, Tex's seatmate, the biker guy, began pushing me around. Something started making me nauseous. It was either the vodka or the spinning, I wasn't sure which, but I had to get off the merry-go-round. The alcohol was starting to catch up with me. I rolled myself off onto the ground with a thud. Suddenly, two legs jumped over me, and a second later, two legs jumped over me again. I moved myself to the grass and looked at the merry-go-round to see a drunken cowboy trying to get on, but he was running too fast to hop on. All he could do is run or let go. Soon, he got tired and opted for letting go, half running and half staggering into the grass next to me. I started laughing at the sight of him.

"I haven't seen anyone do that since I was a kid," I laughed, still laying on the ground.

"It was pretty funny, wasn't it?"

"Yeah, it was," I answered.

I was just starting to feel a little better when the spotlight hit us, lighting all of us up like it was daylight.

"Park's closed. Clear out now," a rather ominous voice announced from the darkness.

I didn't need an introduction, and neither did anyone else. We all picked up our stuff and made a beeline out of the park. Tex grabbed the pizza box and the Frenchman grabbed the bottle, securing it in his bag. The five of us left the park and the officers turned the light off with no incidents. I was glad to get away from them.

"That was close," I said to no one in particular.

"I would have given them one," Tex boasted.

"You would have given them a reason to give you the right to a phone call," the Frenchman said, cutting him off.

    We arrived back at the bus station just in time to catch the bus to Salt Lake City. Woody was standing outside the bus talking up some girl. Noticeably, he had a lit cigarette in his hand, but he never smoked it, instead waving it around like a stage prop. The girl was completely engrossed in what he was saying.

    "You guys have a good time?" he asked me.

    "I'll tell you on the bus," I answered, making my way past him and onto the bus. I worked my way toward the back and sat down. The Frenchman walked past me with the girl in tow, and they sat down in the back of the bus together. The Einstein brothers, cowboy and biker, sat in front of me once again. Woody came along after a few minutes and sat next to me.

    "You look a little under it. That cheap liquor getting to you?" he asked.

    "No, must have been the pizza," I lied, smiling.

    "Yeah, okay. What happened out there? I saw the police car."

    I relayed the story to him, and he laughed at the idea of me on the merry-go-round.

"Pretty stupid, kid."

"It was one of those things that seemed like a good idea at the time."

It was right about then that Tex spoke up with what must have been a bitter revelation to his eyes and in his mind.

"Just look at those two back there."

I pulled myself around to see what was going on behind me, as did Woody and biker Einstein. The Frenchman and the girl were making out hot and heavy in the back of the bus under a blanket. I had no idea where the blanket had come from, but they were putting it to good use. I couldn't tell for sure, but it looked like she had taken her shirt off.

"After I bought the Vodka and paid for the pizza, he gets to do that. How ungrateful can you be?"

Woody looked at him. "First, we pitched in on the pizza. Second, did you want to make it with him?"

"Don't be disgustin'. She was supposed to be my girl. She had it for me until he came along. Don't you remember?"

"Oh, yeah… No," Woody answered him.

I grinned, not being able to help myself. I turned back around and sat down. Woody sat back in his seat, too.

The other Einstein spoke up to Tex, "She's probably got some sort of French social disease now. Just forget her."

Tex agreed with him and sat down, but not before sending what was supposed to be a menacing look to the young couple in the back.

CHAPTER FIVE

The ride to Salt Lake City was uneventful for the most part, partly because each of us was hungover, and partly because there was a limited amount to talk about. With the bus being so quiet, I had some time to reflect on my friendship with Ron, also known as the Americana Man.

We met in school as kids and had a common love of music. Bruce Springsteen, Blue Oyster Cult, and Bob Seger, just to name a few. We also enjoyed just hanging out. He would grow up to become a radio disc jockey, and I would grow up to be a radio listener. In school, we had found creative ways to get into trouble and it made our friendship stronger. It was never anything serious, because I had no desire to get into real trouble, but we were mostly ridiculous, which he was all for.

One such incident took place in gym class. We had an instructor who would teach swimming techniques without ever stepping into the pool. The teacher, who was a really nice guy, never got wet, and we thought we could remedy that. It turned out that part of the swimming class included learning how to get in and out of a canoe, as well as learning how to row. We got in the canoe and pointed it diagonally, right to where he was standing. Both of us rowed as fast as we could until we arrived at the other side, effectively beaching the canoe with a splash on the opposite corner of the pool, getting this guy soaked.

"You two boys! Out of here! Now!" he bellowed.

We got out of there in no time and, luckily, didn't get in trouble for our stunt. It seems it was the first and only time he ever got wet. We left school for the day, and Ron blasted AC/DC on his radio inside the local Montgomery Ward's as we walked through. I think it must have been easier to ignore us than to say anything.

Another time, we held a funeral for a fly I had killed in our math class. It was disruptive, but funny. Ron acted as the minister, giving last rites to the fly, and I acted the part of mourner for this bug.

"Henry was a good fly," Ron announced. "He took care of his wife and maggots at home. He would often bring them the garbage that no other fly would touch."

"He will be missed," I chimed in. "There was no other fly like him."

"He is gone forever," Ron said, holding him up on a piece of paper. "Let us remember that all life is precious."

I opened up a window, and Ron proceeded to dump the fly outside.

"Goodbye, Henry."

Ron then flipped the paper over, dumping the "dead body" out.

"Goodbye, Henry," the class repeated.

The class sat down and everything else went on normally until the bell rang. I later asked the substitute teacher why she never stopped it or said anything. She told me it was so stupid, but in a funny way. She wanted to see it play out, curious about what we were going to do. She also said it wasn't really hurting anything. The fly might have had a different opinion.

As we got closer to Salt Lake City, the bus driver stopped along the side of the road so we could view a waterfall. It's one of the highest in the country, he stated proudly. The stop wrecked my train of thought, but it gave the Frenchman and the girl time to come up for air.

"That is pretty cool," Woody said.

I had to agree. The top of the waterfall was impossible to see because of fog, and it was such a long way up. The bus driver started the bus again, and Woody and I chatted some more. He told me that when we got to Salt Lake City, he wanted to check the local labor board for work he might find there. I thought it couldn't hurt and encouraged him to do so. Salt Lake City was where our little group of travelers would be going separate ways, with the exception of Woody and I, unless he thought he could find work there.

"I've got a question for you, if you don't mind?" I asked him.

"Go ahead. What is it?"

"When we were leaving Omaha, I noticed you smoking. It's the only time I've seen you smoke. What's up with that?"

"Well, it's all about meeting women."

"How's that?"

"Women are people. People like people like them. That's just the way it is. If you want to spend time with them, you've got to be like them. I always carry a cigarette lighter and a pack of cigarettes with me. Someone usually needs a smoke or a light. It's an excuse to talk to them. You ought to try it. You never know when it'll come in handy."

"That really works?" I asked him.

"It's worked so well that it's gotten me a place to sleep and a little more, if you know what I mean."

"Really?"

"Everyone wants someone like to them and someone to be like them. At the next stop, buy some and keep them on you. You'll see what I mean."

"All right, I will."

I sat back and slept for a while. When I awoke, Woody was crunching on crackers. He offered me some, which I gladly took. I asked him where he got them and he said that while I was napping, the bus stopped. He had gotten them at one of the stores near the stop. I was surprised that I didn't wake up when the bus stopped, but I had been pretty tired, so I didn't dwell on it.

We arrived in Salt Lake City early in the afternoon, and the driver instructed everyone to leave the bus because this was the last stop. Everyone got up, checked their seats for stuff, and got off the bus.

I said goodbye to the Einstein brothers, and Tex told me that if I was ever down his way, I should look him up. I told him okay, but I honestly had no idea which way that was. The Frenchman just said goodbye to everyone, including the girl he'd spent so much time lip-locked with, and hopped on another bus. She didn't look amused and walked away without saying anything. Woody gathered up his belongings and asked which bus I was going to be on. I told him the early evening, as I wanted to explore and go see the Mormon Tabernacle.

"Well, maybe I'll see you and maybe I won't. Take care and stay out of trouble. I've got to rent a locker, because I'm not carrying this stuff everywhere."

"I hope to see you later then, but good luck anyway."

I wasn't sure where I was going, but my first priority was the restroom and my second priority was to find a drink. The crackers Woody gave me were good, but they had made me thirsty. The restroom was clean and surprisingly unoccupied, so I took advantage of the emptiness to wash up a little, using the restroom's paper towels as washcloths and towels. I'm sure I stunk, as I hadn't showered in a while. What I wasn't sure of was if the pink dispenser soap was really doing me any good. Like my restroom wash up before, it replaced my body odor with a generic pink soap smell, for good or for bad.

After using the restroom, I found a newspaper stand and bought a soda. It tasted amazing. It was cold, sweet, and fizzy, just what I needed. My needs met for now, I decided to look for the Mormon Tabernacle. I had no real idea what it was or why I should see it, but I knew Salt Lake City was famous for two things: the Great Salt Lake and the Osmond family. The Osmond's were Mormons and the Tabernacle was here. Maybe Donnie and Marie would be there, but I kind of doubted it. I decided to ask the guy at the newsstand how to get there. He gave me directions and I was on my way.

It turned out that the Mormon Tabernacle was more than just the Tabernacle. It was an entire square consisting of about ten acres and the Tabernacle was just a part of it. It is open to the public and, according to what I was told, you can hear a pin drop just about anywhere inside. No one was singing while I was there, but the whole area was interesting to look at. At the time, I was suddenly nervous about talking to anyone there. I wasn't sure why. Maybe it had been one too many after school specials about religious cults. As it turned out, everyone was polite, and no one tried to brainwash or enlist me, making the memory slightly humorous.

There was a lot to see in the square, and one of the most amazing sights I saw was the main temple, or The Salt Lake Temple. It looked like a medieval castle in the center of a modern city. As I looked at the temple, the sun glowed behind it like a halo. I'm sure it was intentional, and it created a gorgeous effect.

I continued to look at the brochures and learned about the square and the Mormons. Joseph Smith founded the church, which has extensive genealogy records in their library and is much larger than I had imagined. I spent my afternoon taking pictures and wandering aimlessly through the grounds.

Fountain Tabernacle Square

By early evening, I'd had my fill of looking around and went back to the bus station to double check my scheduled departure for Seattle. It was sooner than I had remembered, so I was relieved that I had double-checked. I still had a little time, so I found a sandwich shop and grabbed something to eat. The restaurant had free refills on drinks, so while the waitress wasn't looking, I refilled my soda bottle for the road. She must have thought I was awful thirsty. I paid for my meal and left. I tried not to eat at restaurants very often, but occasionally, I needed real meals, not just the snack items I was getting by on.

Walking back to the bus station, I saw a familiar

face. Woody.

"How did you make out?" I asked.

"Mark, I'm getting on the bus with you here in a few minutes. They didn't have anything for me and they ask too many questions."

"Well, I'm sorry it didn't turn out, but I'm glad to see you."

"I guess I'm off to Seattle with you."

"It could be worse."

"Yes, it could. There's always jail."

Traveling with me or jail. Some coin toss. With that, we walked into the bus station and to our bus. As we got on, the driver asked to see our tickets. This was strange, because so far, no one else had really asked. We both produced them and he told us, "Thank you for travelling Greyhound. Enjoy your trip."

So far, so good.

CHAPTER SIX

The ride to Seattle was quiet, with the Einstein brothers, the Frenchman, and the Girl all gone. The Frenchman and the Girl hadn't said much, but they were a source of antagonism for Tex and a source of entertainment for us. That made for a pretty fast trip.

On the way to Seattle, Woody and I chatted a little bit more about his personal life. He was interesting to listen to and would effortlessly go from one story to the next. He had worked as a farm hand, in a saw mill, and done various other rural jobs. He disliked large cities, offices, lawyers, and jail. It seemed like his likes were mostly women and the rodeo. Honestly, though, both took their toll on him.

Being on the rodeo circuit had given Woody a shot at some sort of fame. It was like the cowboy version of a rock star, complete with rodeo groupies called buckle bunnies. After winning the first time, he wanted to keep going. His body had other ideas. Broken bones, torn muscles, and other assorted ailments eventually forced him to stop. All of that, combined with his experience with women, made him a living country song.

We reached Seattle pretty quickly. It would be night soon, and the sky was overcast. Woody asked me what my plans were and I told him I was going to try to get ahold of my friend, Ron. He told me he'd hang out for a bit and wait with me, just to make sure I got ahold of Ron. I called from the bus station, but I got no answer. He didn't know I was coming, so I couldn't expect him to be home. Frustrated, I put the phone back on the receiver.

"So, what are you going to do now?" Woody asked.

"I'm not really sure. Maybe try again later."

"I'll tell you what. I saw a hotel from the bus that isn't too far away. What do you say we get a room with two beds and split the cost? That'll let me get a hot shower, and you, too. I'll even spring for a six pack."

"Sounds good, if it doesn't cost too much. I've got limited funds."

"It's settled, then." Woody gathered up his gear

and we started walking toward the hotel. On the way there, I noticed a very fancy hotel. It was the first time I had ever seen a hotel with a uniformed doorman, like he was in the movies. I watched as he opened car doors for people and then opened the hotel door for them.

"The other half lives pretty good, don't they, Mark?"

"I guess they do. That's some hotel."

As I watched the hotel, a limousine pulled up. The driver got out of the car and opened the door. A small Asian man, dressed in an expensive looking suit and carrying a briefcase, got out of the limo. He walked around to the other side and a very attractive, very blonde woman got out. She was quite tall and dressed in sexy attire.

"How did *that* guy get a girl like that?" I asked Woody.

"She's what they call a call girl. You ever heard of one before?"

"Only in the movies."

"This isn't Hollywood, but I'd bet you anything he's paying for her."

"She's hot."

"And way out of your price range."

As he was speaking, he started looking at street signs, and then he paused for a minute. Woody asked me to watch his things and he said he'd be right back. He crossed the street and went into a drug store. When he came out after only a few minutes, he walked up the street and became obscured by traffic. I stood around and watched the hotel for another glimpse of the blonde beauty, but by then, she and her friend had presumably gone inside for the evening. After a few minutes, Woody was suddenly standing at my side, as if he came out of thin air.

"Where did you go?" I asked.

"First, I went to the drug store to buy some cigarettes and some mints. Then, I went over to talk to those girls over there," he said, pointing to some girls standing near a bar.

"I said hi to them and asked for directions to the hotel I saw. They asked me if I was a cop. When I said 'No,' they told me what they would do for a hundred dollars. I had to explain I was with you. Then, they just gave me the directions."

"What exactly did you mean when you said you were with me?"

"I told them I had a young guy and I was looking for a hotel that we could stay at."

"That's not even funny, man."

"Listen, you're not my type. I just wanted directions to a hotel without being bothered by hookers. I don't care what they think of me. I'll never see them again."

"Great man, just great." I was exasperated.

"Nobody knows you here. Nobody cares," Woody said, picking up his stuff. "Just look at it as a learning experience. So far, you've learned the difference between hookers and call girls. You've learned a little lie in certain circumstances can save you a lot of trouble. Now, let's get to that hotel before it gets dark."

We walked a few city blocks and came upon the hotel. The hotel reminded me of an old school hotel you would see in a movie. There was a dining room across from the desk where you checked in and an elevator in the lobby that accessed the upstairs rooms. We checked in with no questions. The desk clerk informed us that check out was at eleven and breakfast was served in the dining room until ten.

We took the elevator up to our room. The room was a double with two beds and the window looked out at another building. If I moved just right, I could get a glimpse of the famous Space Needle. There was a TV, and most importantly, a shower.

Woody looked at me and, setting his stuff down, said, "I'm going to get that beer I promised you and I'll be right back. Anything else you want? We could split a sandwich."

"That'd be great."

He wasn't gone long, but while he was gone, I kicked off my shoes and stretched out on the bed. Being in a real bed for the first time in days felt good.

"I forgot to ask you what kind of beer you like, so I bought Budweiser. Hope it's okay. I also bought some chips and an egg salad sandwich to split."

"I'm okay with everything but the sandwich. I'm not really that hungry yet."

I sat up on the bed, drinking the beer and eating the chips. It wasn't much of a dinner, but it would do. Woody ate the sandwich and about two chips. I think he felt bad that I didn't want the sandwich.

"I'll see you later tonight. Maybe in the morning, just before check out," he announced to me.

"Where are you going?" I asked.

"There's got to be a lot of women around here who don't charge for a night's entertainment, if you get my drift. Enjoy your beer." And with that, he slipped out of the room.

Once he left, I made sure the door was locked and grabbed a shower. It was only after my shower that I started to realize how badly my clothes smelled. When I got a chance, I'd have to wash them. After my shower, I drank a few more beers, which filled me up, and decided to get some sleep. I stuck my wallet under the mattress and was out in minutes.

"Mark. Hey. Get your ass up. If we're gonna eat before we go, you gotta get up."

I heard Woody's voice, and after a second or two, I put on my glasses to see him putting on his boots.

"How'd your night go? Find a girl last night?"

"I didn't have any luck at all. This is one screwed up town for picking up women. I don't know what it takes, but I tried everything. I gave up about two-thirty this morning and came back here. I tripped over my stuff and made a hell of a racket. Good thing I didn't want to roll you, you'd have slept right through it."

I got out of bed, went to the bathroom, and got dressed.

"Ready to eat?" I asked.

"Let's go."

We left our stuff in the room and wandered down to grab something to eat. I ordered the cheapest thing on the menu: two eggs and toast. The waiter took our order and brought us coffee.

"Well, Mark, after this we go our different ways. I've gotta look for work, somewhere besides here."

"Where are you going?"

"It's a coin flip. Either north to Vancouver, or south to Sacramento, California. What do you think?"

"I have no idea," I replied, as I sipped my coffee.

Woody took a coin from his pocket and said, "Tails Vancouver, Heads Sacramento."

With that, he tossed the coin into the air. He grabbed it and laid it on his arm.

"Heads. Sacramento," he announced, removing the coin before I could see what it was. "Some decisions are too important to think about. You just have to go where life takes you."

We ate our breakfast and went back to the room. It was just about time to check out, so we headed downstairs to turn in our keys at the desk. The clerk asked if we enjoyed our stay and told us to come again soon. We walked out onto the street and headed toward the bus station. Woody needed to catch a bus, and I needed a payphone. I had forgot to call Ron from the hotel room before we checked out. As luck would have it, Woody's bus was set to leave immediately, so we shook hands and wished each other luck. It had been fun traveling with him, and I hated to see him go, but he had places to see and so did I. Goodbyes suck, even with people you haven't known for that long.

CHAPTER SEVEN

I made my way to a payphone and called Ron. I had tucked his phone number into my wallet, so I wouldn't lose it. The only thing that seemed to leave my wallet is money. I dialed the number and waited. His phone rang and rang. I wasn't going anywhere, so I let it ring for a while. Finally, he answered.

"Hello?"

"Hi, Ron! It's Mark. How's everything this morning?"

"Oh, hey man. What's going on? Can't talk too long, I've got to get to work."

"Well, I was wondering if your offer to stay a few days at your place was still open."

"It is and always will be. Thinking of coming for a visit?"

"I'm at the bus station in Seattle right now. How about a ride to your place?"

"Uh…" he paused a moment, "no shit? I can

come and get you, but it's going to have to wait until later today. Right now, I've got to get to work. Can you find something to do until four or four-thirty?"

"I think so. What do you suggest?"

"I don't know. It's a city, man. There's stuff to see. Just meet me at the bus station."

"Okay. Thanks, man. I'll see you then."

"Later, man," he said, hanging up the phone.

Now I had to find some way to pass the next few hours. I walked out of the bus station and made mental notes of my surroundings. The sky was overcast that day, but there were no signs of the infamous Seattle rains. I knew nothing of Seattle, so I started walking towards the nearest landmark I knew: the Space Needle.

The Space Needle is one of Seattle's premier tourist attractions, looking a little bit like a UFO, only five hundred feet in the air. At the top is actually a fancy restaurant with an observation deck that provides incredible views of the city. Some people go to eat and some go for the views. I just wanted some close up pictures. I'm not one for observation decks; I like my feet on *terra firma*. Mountains, I can handle. Observation decks, not so much.

Space Needle, Seattle, Washington

After getting a few pictures of the Space Needle, I decided that I would work my way to the waterfront. Once I got there, I visited an aquarium, where I spent a few hours learning about the marine life of the Pacific Ocean. When I was done, I sat and tried to figure out if there was anything else I knew about Seattle, other than the Mariners and the Seahawks. Then, it hit me. Led Zeppelin had stayed in a hotel on the water, one where you could fish from your window. I could look for that. It would have been the place to stay the night before. The problem was I didn't have a clue what it was called, so I wandered around until I found someplace that I could find help: a magazine stand.

I approached the man in the stand with my question: "Sir, could you give me directions to a hotel on the water?"

"Maybe. You want a newspaper or something?"

"No, I'm looking for the hotel that Led Zeppelin stayed at. I just wanted to see it."

"You oughtta buy a soda or a candy bar or something to keep your energy up."

"I was just looking for directions."

"You could buy a map of Seattle. I sell maps, and they're good ones, too."

It took me a minute, but I figured him out. If I wanted directions from him, I needed to be a paying customer.

"I'm a little hungry. I'll take a Pepsi and a couple of Snickers bars."

I reached in my pocket, pulled out a five, and

paid the man. Suddenly, both his demeanor and his willingness to talk about the city changed.

"You're looking for the Edgewater Hotel. The Beatles stayed there, too, you know. Not just Zeppelin."

He proceeded to give me directions to the hotel on a piece of notebook paper. It didn't seem like it would be that long of a walk.

"Are you planning on staying there?" he asked me.

"No, I just want to see it."

"Lots of people do."

I thanked him, took a swallow of my soda, and started on my way. I bet he sold a lot of stuff that way. As I was walking, I saw a pay phone, and it dawned on me that I hadn't called home yet. I felt a little guilty and decided to call home, figuring my mom would be home.

I called collect, and my mom accepted the call.

"Hi, Mom. Thought you'd like to hear from me."

"Hi," she answered. "Where are you? Is

everything all right?"

"Yeah Ma, I'm fine. I'm in Seattle right now and I'm looking for the Edgewater Hotel. Just something I wanted to see. What's going on there?"

"Your father's at work and your brothers are at school. What have you been doing? Are you eating okay?"

"Everything's okay. Really. I've met all sorts of people. I've been to Chicago, Salt Lake City, and a bunch of other places. I'm catching up with Ron later today."

"Sounds like you're having a good time. Are you eating enough?"

"Ma, I'm not getting fat, but I'm not starving either."

"As long as you're okay."

"I am."

"You be safe out there. Don't go with strangers."

"I've gotta go. I'll call again in a few days. Bye, Ma."

"Okay, goodbye. Be careful."

With that, we both hung up, and I started down toward the hotel. It was big by my standards, and it was right on a dock at the waterfront. It looked cool and I decided that I'd have to stay there someday. The idea of fishing from my room really sounded like a cool idea to my inner-redneck. I wondered if you got to keep the fish you caught, and, if you did get to keep them, what would you do with fish in your room? I took a few pictures and decided to backtrack to the bus station. As I was walking back, the man at the magazine stand waved and asked if I found it. I waved and hollered that I had and thanked him for his directions.

It seemed to take a lot less time to get back to the station than it did to wander to the Edgewater Hotel. I went into the bus station, found a bench where I could lean up against a wall, and watched people go in and out of the station.

It was getting close to the time Ron was supposed to pick me up, and I began looking for him in the crowd. I wondered if he would remember what I looked like and vice versa. That turned out to be a foolish thought, because as soon as he came in, I knew neither one of us had changed a bit.

"Hey, Ron! How you been man?" I asked, smiling.

"Good. Sorry I had to work over a little. Next time, give a guy a little warning when you come to town, will you? I could have gotten a day off or something."

"Sorry about that," I apologized.

"Let's get out of here. I'll probably get a ticket where I'm parked."

We headed out the door, with Ron leading the way. About a block into our walk, Ron stopped in front of a store. He told me to hang out for a second; he needed to buy some cigarettes, and he'd be right out. So, I waited there, trying not to look like a tourist. It must have worked, because I was soon approached by a group of blonde, skinny guys, wearing jeans and light jackets.

"Excuse me, sir, but could you help us?" One of them asked in a thick Swedish sounding accent. "We seem to have lost our vehicle, and we don't know where to find it."

"Actually, I'm not from around here, but my

friend will be out in a second. I'm sure he'll be able to help you."

"Thank you."

Just as he was talking, Ron popped out of the store. I told him their problem and he turned to try and help them. After a few minutes, he was able to get them on their way.

"Nice guys."

"Did you give them crazy directions?"

"Nah, I had a hard enough time understanding them. They've got enough to deal with."

"That's cool."

Soon, we were at Ron's car, and the first thing I noticed was a huge crack in the windshield.

"Is that legal here?" I asked.

"Only if you don't get pulled over."

We climbed in the car, and Ron lit up a cigarette.

"You can toss your bag in the backseat. So what brings you out here, Webster?"

"Just needed to get away. You know, have some adventure. Thanks for letting me stay. I appreciate it."

"You'll have to sleep on the couch. I don't have any extra rooms."

"That's fine. I've been sleeping in buses and bus stations. A couch would be Heaven at this point. You still working at the hamburger place?"

"Yep. I'll buy you lunch there tomorrow."

"I'd like that. Thanks."

As we drove to his apartment, we passed the Boeing Factory.

"That place is huge."

"My mom works there. A friend of hers is the mother of a guy in the band Queensryche. I got to see them rehearse and got some autographs."

"What were they like?"

"Cool enough."

The car started making strange noises.

"I'm afraid The Shitty Blue Maverick is on her last leg. I think the tranny's going," he said, tapping the dashboard. "There are some tapes there on the floor if you want to listen to music."

I saw Tom Petty, Prince, and a band I wasn't familiar with, Los Lobos. Knowing that Ron and I had similar tastes in music, I was curious as to who these guys were. I put the tape in the deck and *How Will the Wolf Survive?* blared through the speakers. I liked it immediately.

"My roommates aren't home, so you'll have to meet them later. I called them and told them a friend would be staying a few days. They were cool with it,"

"I'm glad they were."

"Yeah, I've got decent roommates."

We arrived at his apartment building, got out of the car, and went upstairs. Then we sat down and talked about old times and old friends.

While we were talking, Ron turned the TV on and settled on MTV as background noise. A music video came on for a song called "The Final Countdown." The band featured a bunch of tall, skinny, blonde guys. I looked at Ron and he looked at me.

"Those are the guys we saw downtown."

We found out later they were in town that night for a concert.

"Wish we had asked them for tickets, but then again, we didn't know who they were," I joked.

We talked until it was quite late, and I started to feel hungry. I asked Ron if he had anything to eat.

"Not really. My roommate has some Ramen Noodles in the cupboard, if you want them. He probably won't care. Just let him know you ate them."

I went to the cupboard and found the noodles. They looked a little questionable, but beggars can't be choosers. They cooked up fine and tasted okay. We talked about what we would do the next day. He said he had to work in the morning, but he could take the afternoon off. We'd just do whatever we wanted.

Ron headed off to get some sleep and I laid down on the couch. I was out in minutes. The next morning, when I awoke, Ron had already gotten up and gone to work. His roommates still weren't home, and I needed to decide what to do until he was done working. There were two things I needed: breakfast and a shower.

I looked in the refrigerator to see what my options were. I saw carton of milk that I opened and smelled... not good. It was well on its way to becoming something else. Other than that, the refrigerator was empty. Cold, spoiled milk in a bachelor pad, not exactly shocking. Then, I remembered the Snickers bar in my bag. Thankful for the pushy vendor, breakfast would be a Snickers and flat soda. At that point, it was better than nothing.

The other issue was the shower. After I finished eating, I went to the bathroom and hopped in the shower to clean up. I had soap and a wash cloth, so that part was easy enough. After getting cleaned up, I discovered there were no towels in the bathroom. I was dripping like a wet dog. Then, I spied the roll of paper towels. It wouldn't be pretty, but it worked. I dried off and stuffed the trashcan full.

Ron got back from work shortly after noon, and we headed out to the place where he worked. I had a hamburger, fried mushrooms, and a soda. Ron had a burger and fries.

"What do you want to do, man?" he asked.

"I don't know. Go see stuff."

"All right. As soon as we're done, we'll go hit the mall, the fish market, and where ever else."

We finished eating the great burgers and headed out. The mall was just that, a shopping mall. There wasn't a lot I wanted there, but we did have a good time checking out record shops and girls. Next, we went to Pike's Fish Market, a place where they had too much fun with fish. It was a really interactive fish market and they constantly talked to the customers. We wrapped up the day by going to see a play, *Rap Master Ronnie*, by Gary Trudeau. It was in a small theatre and well-performed. Afterward, we went back to his apartment and met his roommates.

The roommates were brothers, and I told them I ate someone's Ramen Noodles. No one seemed to mind. They had all sorts of questions for me about traveling around the country. Where did I sleep? What did I eat?

Then, the one brother asked, "Why? What's the point?"

"It started off as a way to get as far away as I could from an old girlfriend. But I realized pretty quickly that wasn't the only reason. This guy I met, Woody, told me while we were talking that it's a catalyst that gets things started, but the real reason for taking off is that you are going toward something and not running away. I think I know what he meant. I wasn't really doing this to get away from her; I was doing it because I wanted some adventure and to see things. The situation with my ex just pushed me to finally do it."

"Sounds like you've met some interesting people."

"I have so far."

"How long do you plan on traveling for?"

"A month… or until I run out of money."

"Where are you going next?"

"I'll be here until tomorrow night, and then I'm heading down to someplace in California."

"You've got more nerve than I do."

"Sometimes it's not nerve, it's just not knowing any better."

We talked a while longer, and then everyone started to head to bed. Ron and I discussed going to a

Seattle Mariners' game. I asked him if we could get cheap tickets. He said the way they had been playing, every ticket would be cheap.

Myself, Ron, and my "luggage"

The next morning came, and Ron's roommates' mom had sent over doughnuts for breakfast, a welcome treat. We headed out for the King Dome, where the Mariners played, to watch them play against the Oakland A's.

It became fast apparent that we were not surrounded by A's fans when no one seemed to like that I hollered for Reggie Jackson, who was now in the twilight of his baseball career. I had grown up liking him as a New York Yankee, and since I had never seen the Yankees play in person, I was at least happy to see him. The highlight for me was when he hit a triple, staggering and stumbling into third base.

"Do you think he heard me hollering, Ron?"

"I don't know, but everyone else here did," he laughed.

We filled up on hot dogs and watched the rest of the game, which the Mariners ended up winning. After the game, we back to Ron's apartment, so I could gather up my stuff to leave. He was going to drop me off at the bus station on his way to a concert. Ratt and Poison, two heavy metal bands, were in town that night. Ratt was known for a hit song, "Round and Round," and had a new album out called *Dancing Undercover*. Poison had a hit called "Talk Dirty to Me."

"I wish I'd known you were coming, I would have bought you a ticket."

"That's okay. I've got to get moving anyway. I've got a time limit on this bus ticket, and there's still a lot I want to see."

He dropped me off and we told each other

we'd stay in touch. I walked into the bus station and asked the agent when the next bus leaves for San Francisco. She told me I still had about twenty minutes, so I found a seat and waited. Mostly, I wondered what was to happen next. Seeing Ron was a plan. Now, I didn't have one.

CHAPTER EIGHT

When it came time to leave, I got on the bus and stared out the window, cluelessly thinking about what I should do next. I watched the people and traffic as the bus driver skillfully maneuvered through the city. For a brief second, I thought I saw Ron, but it turned out to be someone else. I counted my money in my head and realized it was dwindling faster than I would have liked. I was okay for now, but I would have to be aware and limit my extra activities.

The bus traveled for a couple of hours, and I dozed on and off. After hanging out with Ron, I was bored, and no one on the bus was talking. It was a very different group of people than earlier in my trip; they just sat there minding their own business. Even Tex would have been a welcome break from the monotonous silence. If nothing else, the silence let me think about everything that had happened so far. When we reached Portland, about three hours later, I decided I wanted more adventure. I made the decision to hitchhike. I got off the bus and started walking south through the city. The weather was decent, and I made pretty good time winding my through the workings of the city. I knew I couldn't hitch in the city, so I decided to wait until I walked to the outskirts.

Once I got out of the city, I started walking with traffic and stuck my thumb out. With hitchhiking, I've found over the years, some days it's all working for you and other days it's not. I walked for a few hours along the side of the road and no one even slowed down. So far, the hitch-hiking part of this trip was not off to a good start. Had I been thinking, I would have cared more about the weather and less about being bored. The whole time I had been in Seattle, it didn't rain, not even a drop. That area of the country was, and still is, known for rain. While I was walking, the sky started clouding up. At first, I attributed it to the setting sun, and then the wind started picking up. With the wind came an added dampness in the air. I knew then I was going to get wet. I figured someone would at least see this poor guy walking along the side of the road with his bag and give him a ride. I found out after forty-five minutes or so that they wouldn't. It started to rain harder. Apparently, I was now about as welcome to a ride as a wet, muddy dog in church on a Sunday morning. No one wanted me in their car. Each and every car drove by me. Some slowed down a little, but only long enough to stare at the wet guy walking up the road. I was about soaked through when I had a bout of reason. I decided to give up and walk back. Perhaps I could catch a ride back to the bus station.

I crossed the highway and started walking in the other direction. In my sopping wet state, I came to the conclusion that some of the cars that had slowed down to watch me walk were likely the same ones that had slowed down on the other side. I began cursing them out and cursing myself out. What a stupid idea this was. I was dry on the bus. I was definitely more comfortable on the bus. I could do the whole trip that way. No matter how much I asked the weather to stop, it kept raining. After a very long walk, I was surprised at how far I had actually gone before I reached Portland again. I could have stopped someplace and warmed up, but I didn't. I was mad. I was wet. I just wanted to get out of a state where a wet guy couldn't get a ride. I found my way back to the bus station and went in.

"Wet out there, huh?" the ticket agent said to me, looking up and down at my sorry state of being.

"You have no idea," I mumbled, showing him my Ameripass.

"Where to?"

"San Francisco."

"About two hours. You just missed one."

"Why am I not surprised?"

I turned and headed for the restroom. I had to go, but mostly I wanted to try to find a way to dry off. I took my shirt off in the stall and wrung it out, doing the same with my other clothes. If anyone had walked into the bathroom, they would have wondered what I was doing. Once my clothes were wrung out, I put them back on. I then stood by the electric hand dryer, repeatedly turning it on in an effort to dry up. It was a little better, but not much.

I finally left the bathroom and went to wait for the bus. When it finally came, I got on and promised myself that I wouldn't get any other brainy ideas. As I looked for a seat, everyone gave me a "don't sit by me" look. I wanted to hug each person for just for spite. I finally found one empty pair of seats toward the back. The air conditioning on the bus was chilly, but at least the seat was dry. I took my seat and I looked out the window at the rain, just glad not to be in it.

CHAPTER NINE

I knew the bus ride from Portland to San Francisco was going to be long, because California is such a large state. The ride to the northern border was quiet, mostly because I was still annoyed at myself over my hitch-hiking fiasco and didn't feel like talking. I was mostly dry, but now there were traces of mud on the bottom of my jeans and my clothes had that lived-in look that said they needed to be washed. My clothes weren't the only thing that needed to be washed. I needed another shower.

As we crossed the California border, the bus pulled over and everyone looked at each other. A man in a uniform with a clipboard got on the bus. I looked at him and forgot about my problems for the moment. At least someone on the bus thought he was important, so I kept my mouth shut and listened to what he had to say.

"Does everyone here speak English? If you don't, I have someone here who may be able to help you," he said, walking up the aisle of the bus.

Everyone nodded their heads or said yes.

"I need to talk to you about an invader to our state… something that doesn't belong here."

My next thought was that he was looking for illegal aliens. I smirked, knowing it was the wrong time, wrong place, thinking that this guy was looking for Canadians sneaking into our country. I attempted to cover my face with my hand, but I had been busted. He shot me a very disapproving glance, though he didn't say anything.

"I'm talking about invasive species of bugs, little bugs that get carried into the state by tourists and other irresponsible people. Are any of you carrying fruits or vegetables? If you are, I'm afraid I'm going to have to take them."

It then occurred to me that we had been stopped by the Department of Agriculture's Fruit and Vegetable Police in what must have been a random stop. The only thing anybody brought forth to the officer was a bag of Washington apples.

He held them up for all to see. "This is what I'm talking about. These could be contaminated, which could cost millions of dollars in crop damage."

You've got to love a guy who's gung-ho about his job. He took the apples and left the bus. Within a few minutes, we were back on our way. I almost expected someone to start eating as soon as soon as he left, but no one did.

Riding along, I had imagined California to be one long Beach Boys song. It wasn't. Northern California was full of trees and mountains. Coastal Redwood trees are something worth seeing on their own. They can grow to over three hundred feet tall and be more than twenty feet across. A forest of that scope is amazing to view and made me feel a little humbled.

Watching the scenery made the time go by, but there wasn't the same camaraderie I had previously experience, which made for lonely traveling. I could see why most movies have two main characters. Still, I was enjoying everything. Eventually, the bus went through Oakland and went on to San Francisco.

I got off the bus in San Francisco, not realizing yet that I had some very naïve opinions about the city. My only plan was to go to the fisherman's wharf and Chinatown. As it turns out, the hippies had left almost twenty years prior. I didn't have a clue which direction to go, but I figured San Francisco was like Seattle. If I kept walking, I'd find what I was looking for eventually.

I picked a direction and started walking. I was busy looking around and people watching, when I started noticing a trend: fewer people and more run down houses. Finally, I turned down a street and was walking when I heard a voice coming from one of the buildings. It was a two-story walkup, the type you wouldn't usually pay attention to, but I sure noticed that voice.

"Hey, kid!"

I turned and looked at the building. I tried to see in from the sidewalk, but I couldn't make anything out.

"This ain't your neighborhood, man. Turn around and leave. Go home," a worn-down, sad voice warned.

Suddenly, a weird feeling came over me. Perhaps it was fear, as I actually looked at the neighborhood, or perhaps it was apprehension, as I became aware of my situation. Whatever the feeling was, I turned around with my head down and my tail between my legs like a frightened dog. Not only did I leave that neighborhood, but I walked right back to the bus station. I went to the ticket agent and told her I needed to go someplace.

"Where did you want to go, sweetheart?" she asked.

I thought for a second, "Someplace nice."

"Santa Barbara's nice. Ever been there?" she asked.

"Sounds good. When does the bus leave?"

"Not long. Fifteen minutes or so."

I thanked her and sat down to wait. Someone had left a map of California in the seat next to mine. I glanced at it, looking at the names of the towns between San Francisco and Santa Barbara. I recognized a couple right away. There was San Jose and Salinas, which I recognized from two songs, "Do You Know the Way to San Jose?" and "Me and Bobby McGee." I started to wonder why I was leaving this city, but trusting my gut instead of brain this time, I figured it was probably a good idea to go.

It was soon time to leave and I got onboard. It would take about five hours to get there and I knew it would be dark. I'd have to figure out sleeping arrangements when I got there. Hopefully, the bus station would be open and I could sleep on a bench.

CHAPTER TEN

The ride to Santa Barbara was filled with towns that I recognized by name and the terrain was beginning to look like what I envisioned. It looked like the California I saw in the movies and on TV, including the palm trees and beaches. Arriving in Santa Barbara was like arriving in a resort town. It was a beautiful area, and I could smell the ocean air. The problem was I had no place to sleep for the night. The bus station was closed for the night, which meant travelers bought tickets directly from the drivers. It also meant that I wasn't sleeping there.

I walked behind the building, looking for a place I might sleep. There was a bench, which I assumed was for employees during their breaks, but would be fine to sleep on for the night. The next problem was that I needed to move the bench out of sight. There were some bushes next to the building, so I dragged the bench between the bushes and the building. It wasn't ideal, but it kept me out of sight from any exiting bus passengers during the night. I laid down on the bench and hoped for two things: waking up before anyone arrived for work and staying dry.

I woke up early the next morning, slightly cramped from sleeping on the bench but early enough that no one had arrived for work at the station. I slid the bench back and decided to walk towards the beach. I didn't know where anything was in this town, but I could tell which direction the ocean was. I was looking forward to seeing the Pacific Ocean from the shore.

As I walked toward the shore, I noticed one striking difference between where I had been in San Francisco and where I was in Santa Barbara: this area reeked of money. I found out years later that I had wandered into the mission district of San Francisco, a place I shouldn't have been. The person who told me to leave likely kept me from getting robbed, beat up, or worse. It amazes me how some people will look out for a stranger. To this day, I am glad I listened.

When I arrived at the shore, the sun had come up and it was a beautiful morning. I crossed the road and just stared at the ocean. It was an incredible sight to see wave after wave slapping the shore with the familiarity of two old friends. There were people sail boarding already, but the beach was almost deserted. I ducked under the rail from the sidewalk and walked to the water. The coolness of the ocean breeze was refreshing. I was fully acting like a tourist, taking pictures of the piers and boats, and my actions didn't go unnoticed. I was approached by a man who I assumed to be a homeless guy or a transient. He rubbed his face and hair and looked me up and down, sizing me up.

"Excuse me, sir. Do you have a dollar?"

"For what?" I asked.

"For a poor, down on his luck veteran who could use a coffee."

"Let me check my pockets."

I reached into my pocket and took out a dollar, some change, a tissue, and a wad of lint.

"Let me see what I've got here," I said to him, as I poked around at the collection in my hand,

"Just the dollar, sir."

I was going to give him all of it, but since that was all he wanted, I handed him the wadded up dollar.

"God bless you, sir. Are you from around here?"

"Just passing through."

"Well, good luck and travel safely."

He then turned away and headed for some other people walking on the beach, likely getting more dollars. I watched him for a few minutes and figured he worked the beach and probably makes good money doing it. I continued my walk along the beach for hours, enjoying the surf, sand, and sun. My jean jacket was getting too warm to wear and I shoved it in my bag. For lunch, I grabbed a hot dog from one of the food vendors lining the beach.

Shoreline of Santa Barbara, California

As the day continued, two things came to my attention. The first was that I was getting a terrible sunburn. A young woman with two children pointed this out to me. She offered me some sun screen, which I gladly accepted. It was too little, too late, but I figured it couldn't hurt. The other issue was I had no place to sleep again. I thought about the bench outside of the bus station, but I didn't want to walk that far. I started looking around the beach for a place to sleep. Under the walkway looked like a place that was out of everyone's sight. If I waited until dark, chances were that no one would see me go under there, so it would be a relatively safe place to sleep. I walked the beach until it got dark, just enjoying doing nothing except watching the water and the women. When it finally got dark, I waited until I was sure no one was looking, then I dropped to the sand and went under the walkway. It was darker under there than I had imagined, so I sat in one place until my eyes adjusted.

In a short time, my eyes got used to the darkness and I made myself comfortable. The sounds of the ocean at night on the beach were soothing. The ocean breeze was light and kept the air under the walkway from getting stale. I laid my jacket on the ground and used my bag as a pillow. I stretched out and, looking the silhouetted Pacific shoreline, I quickly nodded off.

I must have been asleep a few hours when I felt something nudge my side. I looked over to see a shoe with a leg attached to it. Attached to that leg was the rest of a police officer. He shined his flashlight at my face, blinding me.

"What are you doing down here?" he asked.

"Sleeping, officer," I replied, still trying to see him.

"You can't be doing that here. What's your name? Where are you from?"

I told him who I was and that I was from Corning.

"Are you a runaway or homeless?"

"No, I'm just out traveling. I stretched out here to watch the ocean, and I fell asleep. Beautiful beach you have, sir."

He looked at me a bit dubiously and shined his flashlight around some more. He then looked at his watch.

"I'll tell you what. If you're just traveling, I'll

give you a choice. You can travel yourself to a local hotels for the night, or you can be a guest of the city. It's your choice, but I'd rather not deal with you tonight."

I was glad he gave me options, because jail was not anywhere in my scheduled itinerary of places to see.

"I'll take a hotel. Which is the cheapest? I'm on a tight budget."

He rattled off a few hotels, while I picked up my belongings. When I was done, he pointed to the sidewalk and I started on my way.

"Good night, officer. Thanks."

He just looked at me and shook his head, "Goodnight."

I walked towards one of the hotels he mentioned. There was a vacancy sign in the window, and the night clerk sat at the desk reading a magazine. I walked over toward him.

"May I help you?"

"I need a room for tonight."

He told me okay and listed off the room rates. I

told him that I needed the cheapest one, as long as it was clean and had a shower. Funny thought, considering I was just sleeping under a walkway on the ground, but if I was paying, I wanted to get clean. He then told me the total.

"Okay, let me get you some money," I told him.

I proceeded to bend down and untie my sneaker. He stared at me, watching carefully, with the strangest look on his face. I removed my shoe, stood up, and took the insole out. Under the insole, I had two fifty dollar bills; they were damp from sweat. I shook them lightly, in an effort to dry them out, and handed him the money. The night clerk took it by the corner, as if he was holding a dirty diaper, and put it under the cash drawer. He handed me my change, the room key, and a list of rules for the hotel. I took them and headed for my room.

The room was neat, and clean. I wanted to go right back to sleep, but I opted for a shower first. It was as I got into the shower I realized how sunburnt I had actually gotten. The night breeze from the ocean had acted as air conditioning and made me feel cooler than I actually was. In the shower, I felt every drop of water at the same time. I managed to finish up and pat myself dry. Even the soft towel hurt my skin. I went right to bed and didn't wake up until I heard the phone ring. I answered with a groggy, "Hello?"

"This is the front desk. Mr. Webster, will you be spending another night with us. Checkout was ten minutes ago."

"Uh, no. Sorry about that. I didn't hear my alarm. I'll be right down."

I got dressed, looking in the mirror at the lobster I now was, and packed everything up. At least I was somewhat well-rested and not arrested. I checked out and walked to the beach. A little restaurant was open and serving breakfast still. I had already spent more than I wanted, but if I ate a big breakfast, I figured I could go the rest of the day without spending much more on food. I ordered eggs, bacon, home fries, toast, and coffee. The waitress was friendly and very pretty. Unfortunately, I wasn't going to be the biggest tipper she'd ever had.

After breakfast, I decided to give my mom and dad a call. It had been several days, and they were probably worried. I found a payphone that looked out at the ocean and dialed.

My dad answered the phone, "Who is it?"

"Hi, Dad. Thought I should call and let you know I'm still alive. How's everybody?"

"We're good. How are you? Here's your mother."

"Hi, honey. Are you okay? Are you eating enough?"

"Yeah Ma, I'm fine. I just had a great breakfast on the beach. Dad doesn't talk much, does he?"

"Not really. Where are you?"

"California. Santa Barbara, to be exact. It's expensive, though. I think I'm heading out today."

"Where are you going next?"

"I don't know. I've always wanted to see Graceland. Maybe I'll go to Memphis."

"That's nice. When are you coming home?"

"I don't know. Not for a little while."

There was a short silence, then I told her I was going to hang up and I'd call again in a few days.

"All right, then. Be careful out there."

"Yeah Ma, I'm Fine"

We said our goodbyes, and I hung up the phone. I had no idea where I was going when I called home, but I did now. I was going to Graceland.

Mark D. Webster

CHAPTER ELEVEN

I walked to the bus station and thought about my next move: Graceland. I was going to Graceland in Memphis, Tennessee. I didn't want to go there directly, because I wanted to see more of the country first. I looked at the map on the wall of the bus station and chose a city. Reno, Nevada, AKA Little Las Vegas. I wasn't up for another big city yet, but Reno might fit the bill. I went to the ticket agent and showed her my Ameripass, and she told me when the bus would be leaving. It was nicer waiting inside than it had been out on the bench.

I soon boarded the bus and saw a pretty girl, sitting near the back, with long brown hair. I made sure to sit across from her. She looked up and smiled, and I smiled back. Then, she started reading again. I decided I was going to meet this girl.

After a few stops, I noticed she got out every now and then for a cigarette. I remembered what Woody had told me. I went and bought some cigarettes and a lighter, putting them in my coat pocket, and thinking I would join this young lady at the next stop.

After a few hours, the bus stopped again, and this time, when she went out for a smoke, I joined her.

"Oh, shit. Do you have a match or lighter?" she asked me when her cigarette lighter wouldn't light.

"I do." And I handed her my lighter.

We stood there, talking and smoking. I faked my way through, trying not to look too foolish. I wasn't really a smoker. If she noticed, she didn't say anything. Woody's scam worked pretty well; I had broken the ice with her.

If hadn't fooled everyone, though. I managed to draw the attention of a middle-aged couple I called the Mitchells. To me, the husband looked exactly like Dennis the Menace's father, Henry Mitchell. At the next stop, when everyone got off the bus for a break, they asked me if I had a minute to talk to them. I said sure, because they seemed nice enough.

"Son, what's your name?"

"Mark."

"Well, Mark, I'd like to give you a little advice

if you don't mind."

"No sir, go ahead. I can't guarantee I'll take it, but I'll sure listen."

"I can't help but notice that, well…" he paused for a moment and gathered his breath, "that you're smoking periodically. Not like a lot of other people. Just now and then. That tells me that you haven't been doing it very long. As someone who used to smoke, I can tell you that you shouldn't get started. It's a dirty, nasty habit."

"Oh, I couldn't agree more."

"What?" he looked at me, surprised.

"I don't really care for it. It's okay, but it's not my favorite."

"But then, why, son?"

"Because as much I don't care for smoking, I do like pretty girls, and that one over there smokes. When in Rome, do as the Romans do."

"That's not a good reason."

"Maybe not at your age, but from my side, it works pretty well. Anyway, thanks for the concern. I've got a young lady to talk to."

With that, I walked away and joined my fellow traveler. She asked me what they wanted.

"He lectured me on smoking. I think he misses his kids."

We talked for a while longer before getting back on the bus. She was now talking to me a lot more and reading her book a lot less. I enjoyed her companionship immensely. She told me she was getting out in Reno and her mom would be meeting her there. She had been in California to visit her sister. I was starting to everyone had a sister in California.

When we arrived in Reno, she told me goodbye and gave me a quick hug. I was no Frenchman, but I was making progress.

Once in Reno, I realized something that hadn't been an issue so far… I didn't bring any ID. I tried to go into a casino to play the penny slots, and when the doorman asked to see my ID, I couldn't give him anything. That meant he couldn't let me in. I found a ten cent slot machine at a gas station and put a few dimes in, until I got chased away from that, too. My trip to Reno was over as soon as it started, because I couldn't prove that I was old enough to do anything. I boarded the next bus and headed to Memphis.

CHAPTER TWELVE

The ride to Memphis was painfully quiet. I slept and looked out the window, making mental notes of where I didn't want to go. It was about four o'clock when the bus stopped, and I walked into the bus station. They had lockers for rent, so I put my bag in a locker and walked over to the information booth in the station.

"How do I get to Graceland?" I asked the woman at the counter.

Without looking up, the woman answered with the tone of someone who'd been asked this question too many times, "Local bus, Union Avenue."

"Where do I…"

"Out front," she said, cutting me off.

She knew the answers before I asked the questions. I walked out through the door and waited by a sign that said "bus stop." It wasn't long before the city bus came along and I got on. I walked to the back of the bus and found a seat. It was then that I realized I had no idea where I was going on this bus. I would have to watch for something that looked like Graceland. Union Avenue was pretty worn out, and I thought that Elvis couldn't have lived here. As I rode along, I saw all sorts of tourist traps and knew I was getting close. Finally, in the distance, I saw one of the Meccas of Rock and Roll: Graceland. I had arrived.

On my way off the bus, I asked the driver what time the route returns. He told me that this was his last run of the day and he would be back in the morning. This brought up another problem for later. I could only hope to remember how I got to where I was.

Graceland Mansion, Memphis, Tennessee

I headed straight for the ticket booth, only to

find out I missed the last tour by a few minutes.

"Is that the tour bus making its way up to the mansion now?"

"Yes, sir."

"What if I pay you for a ticket, run across the lawn, and get in line before the last old lady gets off the bus?"

"I'm sorry, sir. I can't let you do that. Security would never let you get that far."

"Well, that really stinks. I suppose Elvis isn't home either?" I said, dryly.

"Sir, Elvis is always home. He's buried there. I can sell you tickets to see Elvis' tour bus and his planes, the Lisa Marie and the Hound Dog."

"Thank you. I came a long way to see something."

I toured both planes and the bus; they were lessons in extravagance. Everything was gold this and gold that. There were stories of how Elvis flew to get fried peanut butter sandwiches. As I was leaving either the tour bus, an employee was removing one of Elvis' stage costumes from a display.

"Taking home a souvenir?" I joked.

"No, they just have to be cleaned every now and then. A lot of people go through here."

"That's cool," I replied.

"Are you a big Elvis fan?" he asked me.

"I'm a fan," I answered cautiously. "Why do you ask?"

"Would you like to touch it?" he asked me, looking around.

"Touch what?" I asked him, not sure if I really liked where this was going.

"The jumpsuit, of course. Fans never get to touch anything that the King wore. If everyone touched it, there wouldn't be anything left."

He held the suit out, so I could touch the sleeve. I reached over and felt it. It felt like cloth to me.

"Pretty cool, huh?" he asked me, smiling.

"Definitely cool."

"Don't tell the people at the desk that I did this

for you. It can be our secret."

"No problem. Thanks for doing that."

"You're welcome. I like to help out the fans."

I walked out, not sure what think of the "special" moment. It was just clothes. After that, I decided that if I couldn't go into Graceland, I could at least get some pictures of it. I crossed the street and walked over to the iconic gates. The house seemed normal, like a house with a big lawn. Using my disposable camera, I wanted a good photo, so I walked past the gates and started across the lawn in order to get close photo. A security guard came running out to intercept me.

"Sir, I'm afraid you'll have to get on the other side of the wall."

"I just wanted a picture," I protested.

"Sir, you can take all the pictures you'd like from over there. I'm afraid I'll have to ask you to leave the property immediately."

"Okay, but Elvis wouldn't have cared."

I turned around and walked out through the gates under the watchful eye of the security officer. I wanted to brag that I got to touch Elvis' clothes, but I didn't.

In front of Graceland, a stone wall lines the sidewalk. The wall is covered with all sorts of small, written messages and signatures. I read those for a while, and most consisted of "We love you Elvis" or "So and so was here." I took out my camera and started taking pictures. From the sidewalk, the house is a respectable looking estate that must have made him happy. As I was taking pictures, a guy approached me and asked if I would take his picture in front of the gates of Graceland. I told him I would, and we walked to the gates.

"Did you go inside?" he asked me.

"No, I didn't get here in time, and I'm only in town for one day."

"I didn't either. Have you ever been to Memphis before?"

"No. I got into town and this is the first place I wanted to see. Have you been here before?"

"Yes, and there's a lot more here than just this. This town is loaded with stuff to see."

"Like what?"

"Like, I've got a few Coronas in my car. Want a beer and I'll tell you?"

A beer sounded good to me, so I agreed. We walked over to his car. It was a small hatchback that was packed full with clothes, a sleeping bag, food, and other things. He noticed I was staring at it.

"Man, I have been living in my car and traveling for weeks. Just came back from New Orleans. All kinds of good music."

"Sounds good to me."

"Have you ever been there? I was there for Jazz fest and Mardi Gras. It's an amazing place," he said, as he opened his hatch and handed me a beer. "There's everything anyone could want to see or do."

He opened his beer with a bottle opener and tossed the opener to me. It wasn't super cold, but it wasn't warm either.

"Sorry I don't have any limes."

"That's okay. How'd you end up here?" I asked.

"I'm just traveling around. I look for a place

that has whatever music interests me, and I go there. Went to some Grateful Dead shows, a few other bands. Mostly I look for bands like Los Lobos."

"I've heard of them. A friend of mine is into them."

"I really like good music, not the stuff you hear on the radio."

"I ought to introduce myself. My name's Mark. You are…"

He stuck out his hand and said, "Mike. Nice to meet you, Mark. Now, where are you headed?"

"I'm not really sure. I've got to go back to the bus station to get my bag. Could I trouble you for a lift?"

"I'm not sure. I don't usually pick up hitch-hikers…"

"I understand."

"I'll tell you what," he paused. "If you don't mind a couple of stops along the way, I'll give you a ride."

"Deal."

He reached into his car and pulled out a few more beers. We sat on the hood of his car talking about music for about an hour. He slid his skinny, denim-clad frame off the hood and decided we should get going.

"First stop on the tour, Sun Records. Sun Records was Sam Phillips' record label, the original home to Elvis, Carl Perkins, and Johnny Cash, to name a few."

He slowed up the car and handed me his camera. "Take a picture for me, will you?"

I took the picture and handed his camera back. He sped up the car and said our next stop was a hotel. I gave him a funny look.

"It's not what you're think. This is the Lorraine Motel, where Reverend Martin Luther King Jr. was killed in 1968. Now, sit there and be quiet for a minute. Just listen," he said, rummaging around for a cassette tape.

He soon found what he was looking for - a cassette of the Irish band U2. He put the tape in the stereo and turned up the volume. The song, "MLK," came through the speakers. I listened to the singer and watched Mike, who looked as if he was in church.

When the song was over, he said, "Amen." Then, he turned and looked at me, so I said the same.

"Let's go inside," he suggested.

We walked up the stairs to a small room, where there was a memorial to the Reverend and a small can for donations. We each put some money in the can, and without saying a word, we walked around the room to examine the small exhibit. Before we left, Mike made the sign of the cross and said a quiet prayer.

Lorraine Motel, Memphis Tennessee

As we walked to the car, an old man wearing a dingy white t-shirt and black dress pants stopped us. He told us how he had been there that day and saw everything that happened. He talked for about fifteen minutes or so, and then Mike told him we needed to leave. He asked us if we could help him out with some money, because he was on hard times, so we each gave him a dollar. He thanked us, lit up a cigarette, and went and sat down on a curb.

We got in the car, and Mike said we were headed to the bus station to drop me off. The trip only took a few minutes.

"Thanks for the ride and the tour. Oh, and the beers."

"You're welcome. Where you going next?"

"I'm thinking New Orleans. See you someday, maybe."

"Doubt it. Take it easy and be safe."

With that, I watched him roll up his window and drive away. I remember that my dad had given me the number of a friend whose son lived in New Orleans, so I knew where I was going next. Louisiana, here I come.

Mark D. Webster

CHAPTER THIRTEEN

I went into the bus station and retrieved my belongings from the locker, before finding out when the next bus was leaving for New Orleans. It was going to be about an hour, so I found a bench and sat once again. The trip was going to take about 6 hours, which wasn't really that long, but I had enjoyed riding around with Mike and didn't really feel like riding the bus. Forgetting what I had told myself, I decided I would try my hand at hitch-hiking again, getting out at the first stop outside of Memphis. The bus came and I got on. Everyone on it was quiet, and the hour I sat riding went by uneventfully. When the bus stopped, in a town I can't remember, I got off. Making sure to hit the restroom first, I started walking in the same direction as the bus.

The evening air was cool and traffic was slow. I leveled my thumb, and twenty or cars must have gone by me before one finally stopped. It was a sedan with an older man behind the wheel. He was dressed in a suit, but his tie was loose.

"Where you going, son?" he asked me.

"New Orleans, sir."

"I'm not going anywhere near that far, but I can give you a ride for twenty miles or so."

"That would be great. Thank you," I said, climbing in the car.

As he pulled onto the road, he asked, "What sends you to New Orleans?"

"I wanted to travel. Get away from things at home. See some stuff."

"Oh, you'll see stuff there," he chuckled.

"How about you?" I asked him. "What do you do?"

"Oh, I work for the Lord," he smiled. "I've got a little church and we go up to Memphis to help those people out. There's a lot of downtrodden folks up there."

"I was just in Memphis. Interesting place."

He looked at me for a moment and said, "It's home to two of the biggest tragedies in this country. One man who had it all and one man who gave it all. Heartbreaking. Absolutely heartbreaking."

He asked if I went to the Lorraine Hotel, and I said that I had. I told him about the man who said he was there the day Reverend Martin Luther King Jr. was killed.

"Every old man in Memphis will tell you that. It must have been an awfully crowded place."

I was surprised that he put it that way, and I continued listening.

"Someday, they'll have a proper memorial. I've looked into it and they say it's coming. A man's work is his legacy and his is already bigger than any building." Years later, I can still hear him telling me this.

We rode on for a while, with him asking me about my family and me asking about his work. It wasn't long before he pulled the car off to the side of the road.

"This is where you are getting out. Mark, it's been a pleasure talking with you. Good luck and God bless."

"Thank you, and you, too."

I waved at him as he drove off. If every ride was going to be like that, I'd never take the bus again. I started walking again and stuck my thumb out. A few cars went by without slowing down. I walked for almost an hour and there was almost no traffic, which seemed odd for a "busy" highway. Then, as I looked down the highway, I saw a car slowing down as it approached me. It wasn't just any car; it was a very large Cadillac. This was going to be a sweet ride. The car stopped next to me and the passenger's side front window rolled down.

"Where you headed?"

"New Orleans."

"I am, too. Come on and get in."

I opened the heavy door and sat down. The driver looked me over and told me to buckle up. Then, he started back onto the highway.

"What's your name and where are you from?" he asked.

"My name is Mark and I'm from Corning, New York."

"Ah, a Yankee boy. Pleasure to meet you. I'm Brother Walter from the Jesus is Going to Rock Your World and Save Your Soul Church. This is my holy vessel. I'm on my way to start a new church in New Orleans or someplace there about."

Looking at him, I immediately got the impression of a mix between Little Richard and a used car salesman. This guy was slick.

He continued, "I've been on the radio, in the pulpit, and on the minds of sinners everywhere. Have they heard of me in Corning yet?"

"I'm going to guess no."

"Oh, they will someday, if the Lord wills it."

As we kept driving, I noticed that the interior was pristine. This car looked like it just rolled off the lot, with two exceptions. There was a plastic Jesus on the dashboard and the tape deck was not factory. This man liked his music. I thought that might be a good talking point.

"Walter, what kind of music do you like? I couldn't help but notice your stereo system."

"It's Brother Walter. I like all sorts of music. I have to tell you though, the tape deck is so that I can hear myself."

"Hear yourself?" I said, not really

understanding what Brother Walter was talking about.

"Yes, hear myself. Go ahead and open the glove box. Put one of those tapes in the player.

I did what he said, placing a cassette in the tape deck. Brother Walter reached over and turned up the volume.

"You're going to like this," he said, smiling.

The tape player whirred, and I heard the sound of somebody tapping a microphone. After a moment of this, I heard an organ playing. It didn't sound like a church organ, but more like the one you would hear at a baseball game. The music started and I heard a high-pitched woman's voice. The tape went something like this:

"Listen up, everybody. It's time for Brother Walter's Old Time Sunday Gospel Show. Now for your servant of the Lord, Brother Walter," the squeaky voice announced.

"Thank you, thank you," Brother Walter spoke into the microphone. "I am Brother Walter, and you are listening to Brother Walter's Old time Sunday Gospel Show, featuring me, Brother Walter. I'm going to tell you the Lord's message today."

"Tell us, Brother Walter!" a woman replied.

"Tell us what the Lord has to say today!" another woman said.

"I'm here to save you. Save you from the Devil. Save you from yourself. But to do so, I need you to help yourselves! The Lord helps those who help themselves, and I am going to be the one who helps you do that. You may ask 'How can he help me to help myself?" I'm going to tell you how. It all starts with a phone call and a check. It takes money to be on the air, and the Lord hasn't left his checkbook lying around. I need you to write a check to me, so I can do the Lord's work! Together, we can pay His bills. You send a check today, and I'll pay His bills tomorrow! We're a team for the Lord, but I can't help you unless you help the Lord. "

"We're on your team, Brother Walter," the women chimed in.

"No, ladies. You're on God's team. Can I get an Amen?"

"Amen," they said in unison.

"Amen for God's team," Brother Walter

cheered them on.

"Amen for God's team"

This went on for a solid twenty minutes. Every cliché I associated with TV Evangelists was on full display in this broadcast. Brother Walter left nothing out. When the show was over, I let out a sigh of relief that didn't go unnoticed.

"Sort of takes your breath away, doesn't it?" Walter asked. "Now, flip that tape over."

I did as I was asked.

"I can tell how much you were enjoying that show. I've probably got enough tapes to last all the way to New Orleans."

I looked at Brother Walter and knew he wasn't kidding. The next show started up. As Walter was driving, he began repeating his sermon word for word. It became apparent that he had listened to these tapes repeatedly, as if they were tapes of favorite songs. He also began to act out the tapes, waving his hands around to an invisible audience and looking like he was rehearsing for a play. I watched him with amusement for a while, because he was now driving without his hands on the wheel. This lasted for hours, but I eventually fell asleep as he continued on.

I wasn't sure how long I slept for, but I suddenly felt a hand shaking my arm.

"Mark, wake up. We're here," Walter said, nudging me awake.

"Amen, Brother. Amen," I hollered.

Brother Walter looked at me. "I am going to drop you off at the bus station. That way, if your friends aren't around, maybe you can get a ride somewhere else."

"Thank you. I appreciate it."

"You are welcome," he said, as he pulled the car over. "Now let me get my card, so you can contact me if you need to. I think it's in my wallet. Before that though, I want to warn you about the women in this town. They are trouble. Keep yourself away from them. Stay chaste. That means stay away from women. Did you get that?"

I nodded my head. At that point, Brother Walter opened his wallet and condoms sprung out onto the seat and floor.

"You did not see this and you are to tell no one. Understand?" he said, picking up the condoms from the seat.

I quickly said, "Yes."

"Good. Be safe the rest of your trip," he smiled, rushing me along and forgetting to give me his contact information.

"Thanks for the ride."

I shut the door, which, after a nap, didn't feel so heavy. Brother Walter honked his horn and waved as he pulled out. I wished that I had gotten one of his tapes, but I don't think he would have ever parted with them. I walked into the bus station and sat down. It was too early in the morning to call anyone, so I decided to wait it out inside. I would have to call my dad's friend's son once the sun came up.

CHAPTER FOURTEEN

Once daylight arrived, I decided to make the call. It needed to be early enough that they were home, but not so early that I would wake them up. Seven AM seemed like the ideal time. I walked over to the payphone and took the number from my wallet. Before I dialed, I rehearsed what I was going to say.

"Hi, you don't know me. Can I stay at your house for a few days?"

"Hi. Your dad said you'd let me stay at your home?"

I worked through various versions of the same thing until I decided to call. The first thing I did was call the wrong number. I took a minute and gathered my thoughts and tried a second time. Hopefully, the second time would go better than the first, because the first attempt reminded me how early it was.

A sleepy voice answered the phone.

"Hello?"

"Good morning. My name is Mark Webster,

and I know you have no idea who I am, but your dad told me that if I made it to New Orleans, I should give you a call, and you would let me stay at your house for a few days. I was calling because I'm here and have no idea if it's okay or where exactly you live." I said all of this in almost one breath.

"Hold on a second. My dad said what?"

I explained it to him again, calmly and with a little more detail. He asked me for the number of the payphone and said he'd call back in a few minutes. I thanked him and told him I would be waiting. After five long minutes, the phone rang.

"Hello?" I answered.

"Mark?"

"Yes, this is he."

"I called my dad, and asked him if he knew a Mark Webster and why he was calling my house looking for a place to stay. He started laughing and said he was surprised you made it here, but he was glad to hear you were all right. He told me that he did tell you that and asked me if I could let you stay and show you around. I said I would, so I'll be down to get you in a little bit. First of all, where are you?"

"I'm at the bus station in the city."

"Give me a half hour. Bye." And with that, he hung up the phone.

With a half hour to kill, I went for a walk outside. The humidity was already climbing. I imagined it must feel like a sauna in the afternoon. Traffic was light around the bus station, but that would likely change later. I went back inside where it was a bit cooler and played a game where you could win souvenirs. I managed to win a calculator with a New Orleans sticker on it. Mostly though, I just sat and looked around.

A thin, balding man, sporting a grey beard and wearing a denim work jacket, approached me.

"Are you Mark?"

"Yes. Are you Dave?"

He held out his hand and we exchanged greetings. He seemed instantly likeable.

"I'm going to drop you off at my house, but first I've got to check in at a job to make sure my workers showed up. Do you drive?"

"No. I haven't gotten around to getting my license yet."

"If you drove, I'd let you take one of my work trucks for the next few days. But don't worry, the city has a great transit system. The bus will take you right to the street I live on. You'll only have to walk a half block or so."

"That's cool."

We pulled up to a work site in the French Quarter where several guys were painting. Dave instructed me to stay in the truck, and he got out to talk to his crew. After a few minutes, he got back in and we drove to his home,

"Those guys are a good bunch. JD plays in a band, and sometimes he has a hard time making it to work, so I like to check in. It lets them know I'm paying attention."

"Sounds like a good idea to me."

"How long do you plan on staying? Mardi Gras and Jazz fest have already passed. I'm not sure what you want to see."

"Honestly, I'm just out traveling. I needed to

get way away from an old girlfriend. You know, a little time and a lot of space to rest my head. She was nice enough, but not for me. Sometimes, it takes a while to learn these things. I get it now. Plus, there's a lot to see in this country."

"I was thinking you could stay three or four days," he said, looking at traffic light and seemingly ignoring what I had said. "There are also a lot of women here. If you can't meet someone here, that's pretty sad. I won't worry if you don't come back to the house one evening."

"I'll keep that it mind."

We drove about ten minutes before Dave pulled onto a small street just outside the city. The house, he said, was called a Shotgun Shack, because you could shoot a shotgun from front door to back door and it wouldn't hit anything. I didn't think his home even remotely resembled a shack. It was nicely decorated and very clean. He told me I could sleep on the couch in the living room or upstairs. I opted for upstairs, because I could stay out of the way. He had to go to work, but before he left, he showed me the shower and the washing machine, just in case I wanted to use either. I don't know if that was a hint or just Dave being courteous, but I took advantage of both.

Being clean was starting to seem like a real luxury at times.

After doing a load of wash, everything washed and dried together, I decided to take a nap. I slept until I felt something looking at me. I opened my eyes to see a dog standing on his hind legs, looking me over. As my eyes strained to focus, I felt a wet tongue slide across my face.

"Hi. How are you, pup?" I said, petting the dog.

"I'm sorry," I heard a woman's voice say in the room behind me, "did she wake you?"

"Yeah. No problem, though. I'm Mark."

"I'm BJ. Dave said you were here. Find everything okay?"

"Yes, thank you. I really appreciate you letting me stay here for a few days."

"Dave's father said you were a real good guy, and I like him a lot. It's no problem. Do you want to grab a bite to eat?"

"Sure. What did you have in mind?"

"You'll probably want seafood. I know a place where you can get crawfish, and I can get a salad."

We went to her car and drove to a little place by the waterfront. She ordered me some crawfish and fries and ordered herself a salad. We talked a little bit about the area, and she told me where it was okay to go and where it wasn't. She said that a good rule of thumb was to only go to places with street lights. Then, the waitress brought out the food and drinks.

I looked at my crawfish, then looked at BJ, and asked, "Okay, how do you eat these things?"

She told me to twist them where the tale connects to the back and then pull the tail and suck the head. As I was attempting this, our waitress came over and watched.

"Yankee suck," she giggled.

"What?" I asked BJ.

"Yankee suck. It means that she can tell by the way you're eating that you're a Yankee. It's not an insult, just a fact."

"How do you do it?"

"I don't care for them much, but I'll show you."

She proceeded to break one in half and made a huge slurping noise, then she sucked the head of the crawfish. She handed me the tail, which I peeled like a shrimp.

"Now you try."

I picked up another crawfish and tried to do it like she did. I looked up to see her and the waitress smiling at each, agreeing. "Yankee suck."

"Thanks, ladies."

"Don't feel too bad. We'll go get some beignets with powdered sugar at Café du Monde after dinner."

"What are those?" I asked.

"To you, powered doughnuts."

"Are they expensive?"

"I'll treat. Dave's going to meet us there later."

"That's good."

We sat there for a while, eating and talking about New Orleans. I couldn't quite get a handle on the crawfish head sucking, but they were good nonetheless. We paid our checks and walked around the French Quarter a bit, as Dave had to work for a while longer. I couldn't help but notice the signs in front of the drag bars.

"Some of them are, well… impossible to tell." I fumbled for the right words.

"Some are really pretty," BJ said. "Dave will tell you just to stay away from those places. They're too close to the real thing."

"After too many drinks, I could see that being an issue for some people."

We walked on and I looked for a gift for my mom. I found a ceramic mask. BJ said it was touristy, but that's exactly what I was. The time went by, and I noticed they were blocking off the street.

BJ saw the confusion on my face. "They shut down the streets in the Quarter at night. Everyone walks."

As we were walking, BJ gave me a history lesson on the French Quarter. The outsides of the buildings were often bland, but the insides had beautiful courtyards. We stepped into Pat O'Brien's Bar and Grill, so she could show me what she meant. It was really nice inside, full of lights and greenery. The bar is known for a mixed drink called a Hurricane, made with rum, fruit juice, and grenadine, that the bar's original owner created. We didn't stop for one, but I kept it in mind for some other day. We walked around until it was time to meet Dave. We met him at Café du Monde.

"Hi, you two. Having a good time?"

"I am, Dave. Your wife is a great tour guide."

"Glad to hear it."

We walked into the café and ordered coffee and beignets. The coffee turned out to be espresso, which had a little bite to it. The beignets were served on plates and BJ blew the sugar from mine into my face.

"Now you've been initiated like a local," she laughed.

"Thanks… I think," I said, wiping off the sugar.

"Where do you want to go next?" Dave asked me.

"I don't know. Where ever you guys want to go is fine with me."

"Let's go to Benny's. JD is playing with his

band. We can go see them."

We went back to their house, so they could drop one of the cars off, and we went to a bar called Benny's. It wasn't much to look at, but it was pretty crowded. The band sounded incredible. I recognized JD as the same JD that was painting earlier. Dave asked if I played guitar or anything, because they loved having musicians sit in. I told him I played a little, but these guys were way out of my league. I had a hard time believing that they had to find other jobs in order to make a living. As it turns out, one of the band members was from Buffalo, NY. I guess it really is small world. After a while, we had to leave, because Dave and BJ had to work the next morning. One of the hardest things to do is leave a band when they're on. These guys were on.

The next morning, I rode with Dave into the French Quarter, where I went exploring. I wandered the streets, looking at the architecture, window shopping, and listening to street musicians. One, in particular, was playing the saxophone in a doorway arch. I watched as a little kid walked by and the musician changed his tune. He began playing something that got the kid's attention. "Da dant, da dant" went the first bars of Henry Mancini's theme from the Pink Panther. The kid stood there watching him, taking in every note. Soon, one of the kid's parents took a dollar and placed it in his case on the ground. The kid took it out and put it back in himself, as if to approve. They moved along, and the man shook his head in thanks. Like a magician performing an effortless trick, he slipped back into the original song seamlessly.

I wandered over to the Jax mall, where I ordered crawfish, potatoes, and a beer for lunch. The waitress was a young, pretty, Cajun girl who didn't speak to me much. I did notice her speaking to one of the other waitresses and all I understood was "Yankee suck." Busted, but the food was good. After lunch, I wandered to the Ripley's Museum to get out of the humidity. The museum is a great collection of weirdness and human oddity, plus the air conditioning felt good, so I really took my time.

I located the local bus and headed back to Dave and BJ's house. When I got there, BJ was home and asked if I wanted to go with her to the university. She had some things to drop off and afterward, we could go down to the waterfront. It sounded like fun, so I said yes. On the way to the university, she told me a story about thieves breaking out the passenger's side window of vehicles driven by solitary women drivers.

It had been quite risky driving around the university area. It continued until the thief tried this maneuver on an off-duty police officer and she shot him. The robberies stopped after that. When we got to the university, BJ dropped her papers off and we proceeded to the waterfront. While there, we were approached by a man carrying a can of shoe polish and a rag. He was wearing a pair of slacks, a dress shirt, and a sport coat.

"How are you folks doing today?" he asked.

"We're both good," I answered.

"Glad to hear it. I am as well. Let me ask you a question. Now, are you folks betting people? For a mere five dollars apiece, I will bet that I can tell you where you got your shoes. Are you up for it?"

I looked at BJ and she looked at me.

"It's too good to be true, I know. It's an easy five dollars, but I'm willing to take that chance," he said convincingly.

"Now, wait. You're going to tell me where I got my shoes?" I asked.

"Yes, sir. And the lovely lady too. I will tell you both where you got your shoes, right here and now."

"What do say, BJ? He might guess yours, but I'm not a local."

She looked at me and said, "Why not? It's only five if he does get it right."

"Are you in? You will pay up, right?" he asked.

We both said yes.

He looked at us with a self-satisfied grin, knowing he'd gotten two more suckers. "You got them on your feet, right here and now," he said, as he burst out laughing.

I opened my wallet and paid him. I couldn't help but laugh at myself for being tricked so easily.

.He took the money and put it in his pocket. He then said, "I'll tell you what. I'll polish her shoes for you two being so good about it. You're wearing sneakers, so I can't shine your shoes. I will you give you some advice, though. If someone one wants to make a bet with you and you've never seen him before, tell him no, cause he already knows the outcome. You can't beat the man. There you go. "

With that, he finished polishing BJ's shoes. I looked at her and asked, dryly, "Million dollar shine?"

"Ten dollars, anyway," she said as we walked away.

When we got back to the car, BJ told me we were invited to a crawfish boil in the French Quarter that night. I wasn't quite sure what that entailed, but crawfish sounded good. She told me we were on our way there and Dave would meet up with us.

It didn't take long to get to the French Quarter area, and we parked in a lot. The party was within walking distance and when we arrived, we had to pass through gates to get to a courtyard. The courtyard was beautifully landscaped with a variety of plants and a fountain. Among the plants were two large makeshift tables comprised of saw horses and sheets of plywood. They were covered with newspaper, made to look like a tablecloth. Tubs filled with ice, beer, and soda were scattered on the ground. It was an impressive sight to my eyes.

Dave and another man greeted us as we came in.

"What's the occasion?" I asked.

"We just finished work on this place, and this guy wanted to celebrate with a party at his new home," Dave said, pointing to our host.

"Thank you for letting me tag along tonight. This place is amazing." I said, shaking his hand.

"Oh, you're welcome. Be sure to eat and drink whatever you want."

"Thank you."

I looked around at the empty tables, wondering when we'd eat. I grabbed a beer and looked around some more, while Dave, BJ, and the host chattered on. It wasn't long before several people came out with pots of steaming food and dumped them on the newspapers. There were piles of steaming potatoes, corn, peppers, and crawfish. One of the people came out with plates and napkins, but that seemed like a minor afterthought. At this point, there were about fifty people at this party. They were laughing, drinking, and having a good time. The only disappointing thing was the radio playing top forty and not zydeco music, but I suppose that was my vision.

The party was a great look at how the other half lives. One person I met was a lawyer who referred to himself as "the juggernaut of justice." He told me that if I ran into trouble while I was in New Orleans, I could call him. I didn't want legal trouble, but I thanked him and kept him in mind.

After the party, we went back to the house. I went upstairs to lie down on the couch, when I overheard Dave and BJ talking. They were afraid I was getting bored, but it was quite the opposite. I was having a blast in New Orleans, too much so. I was actually starting to run low on cash, I was getting worn out, and I was thinking it was time to go home. I decided to tell them in the morning.

When I awoke the next morning, Dave and BJ were having coffee. I poured myself a cup and asked if they had a minute. I told them that I was going to leave that night, after I spent the day wandering some more. They were both agreeable, and Dave told me that if I came back that way again, I should come and see them. He also told me to contact him myself and not to rely on his dad to do it, which made us all laugh. Dave finished up his coffee and got ready for work, while BJ and I talked for a while. Dave walked over, offering his hand.

"Mark, it's been nice spending some time with you."

"Dave, thanks for letting me stay and showing me around. You guys have been great. I'll always remember this."

We shook hands and Dave headed out the door for work.

"Mark, I've got to leave in a few, myself. Where would you like to be dropped off?" BJ asked.

"I think I'd like the French Quarter, perhaps Rue or Bourbon Street."

"Not a problem."

She went off to the bedroom, and I went upstairs to pack my stuff. I had washed my clothes while I was there, so I had enough clean clothes for a while. Everything was packed neatly and I wrapped the gift for my mom securely in a shirt. There were no guarantees it wouldn't get broken, but I was going to get an A for effort. We went out to the car and sat down.

"It's been nice having you here. I like having company at the house. Dave's dad was here last year and we had a great time," BJ said, starting the car.

"He's a great guy. He and my dad go to OTB together and bet horses."

We talked about my dad and Dave's dad until we got to the French Quarter. BJ drove me to the end of

Bourbon Street and dropped me off. As I got out, she told me to come back again someday. I told her I'd try, but figured I never would. There are too many places to see and life gets in the way. I waved as she drove off, and I watched her car disappear into traffic.

The next thing I had to do was get my bearings. I can live without knowing where I'm going, but I like to know where I've been. Over the last few days, I had wandered around enough to know where certain landmarks where. The Superdome, the bus station, and Pat O'Brian's were enough to steer me around for the day. I walked the streets, looking at buildings and people. New Orleans is a great place for both. The atmosphere there is like no place else. Sit in a café or walk the street in the rain and you're instantly transported into any novel you could imagine.

By late afternoon, I decided to head back to the bus station. Even though I had hitch-hiked into the city, I was riding the bus back out. I looked at the map in the bus station and picked a route home. I would go to Atlanta, Washington, D.C., Philadelphia, Binghamton, N.Y., and finally, home. It would take a few days, and that was fine. I had been gone almost a month, so a few more days didn't seem like all that long.

Mark D. Webster

"Yeah Ma, I'm Fine"

CHAPTER FIFTEEN

The ride to Atlanta was quiet. The bus was mostly empty, and, for once, I just didn't feel like talking to anyone. I stared at the landscape as the bus drove along the highway and watched as day blended seamlessly into night. In a familiar move, I pressed my head against the window and fell asleep. I would wake up occasionally, as the bus loaded and unloaded people, but, for the most part, I stayed asleep.

When we reached Atlanta, I discovered that I had more than four hour to wait for the next bus. I had gotten used to eating regular meals the last few days, so I was quite hungry. My wallet told me otherwise. I was down to about ten dollars and would have to stretch that out to three or four dollars a day for food. I went to the newspaper stand to see what they had that would hold me over for. I spotted some cheap food: pork rinds. Not exactly my idea of delicious, but at least they would hold me over for a while. I paid the man and found a place to sit down. This ninety-nine cent bag would last me two meals if I was careful not to sit on them or crush them with my bag. I found a bench to sit on and started eating my lunch. I had part of a Pepsi from earlier, so I dug it out of my bag. The pork rinds were salty and made me thirsty, so I drank my Pepsi quickly and continued with the pork rinds. When I finished the soda, I was careful to put the empty bottle back in my bag for water later on. Water, thankfully, was still free from a sink or drinking fountain.

After a while, perhaps an hour, a woman sat down next to me. She was in her mid-forties, average looking, and dressed casually. She was carrying a large purse, which she clung to rather tightly, and no luggage. I noticed that most people carried at least an overnight bag. I said hello and made small talk about traveling by bus.

"Where are you going?" I asked.

"I've got to go meet some people," she replied.

Not exactly the answer I was looking for. I thought I'd try a different approach.

"I was just curious. I'm headed back home to Corning. I was traveling and stopped to visit friends in New Orleans, and now I'm headed home."

"That's nice. Did you have a good time?"

"Yes, I did."

The conversation continued on like this for a while, and she seemed to get comfortable talking to me. She opened up her purse to retrieve a drink when I saw it. She saw that I saw it. She had a pistol in her purse.

"Is that what I think it is?" I asked without thinking.

"Yes, and I'm allowed to carry it."

"I wasn't going to argue with you. You've got the… you know."

"Okay, I wasn't going to tell you this, but I'm a US marshal. I'm going to meet up with another officer."

"You don't have a patrol car?"

"I've got to meet up with another officer, and we're carpooling to pick up someone. I offered to bus in, because the other officer was coming in from the opposite direction. That way I didn't to leave my car."

She showed me her badge quickly.

"It's really cool who you meet traveling like this."

She looked at me. "Please keep this quiet. I don't need everyone knowing."

"No problem. I think it's cool. I'm the safest person in this place."

"My bus is leaving in a minute. Have a safe trip home."

"Thanks, you too."

I watched as she headed out the door and to her bus. That was pretty cool. I sat and waited around for another hour or so until my bus was leaving. I got on the bus, and they checked my ticket. Not every driver did this, so it was weird that this one did.

"One more day left on your pass. Did you notice that?"

"I didn't notice. Thanks."

I had to wonder how far I wasn't getting. Fortunately, most of the drivers didn't check too closely, so I might be able to make it back to Corning on the bus. I could hitch-hike the rest of the way if I had to.

The next day was quiet, and the next major

layover was in Washington D.C. I waited around in the bus station for a while, and then I decided to wander outside. There was an increased police presence outside the station, and I asked an officer what was going on. He told me that President Reagan was across the street. The secret service was all over, so I might want to go back inside. I took his advice and went back in. While I was sitting on one of the benches, a college student sat down next to me and we started talking. I told him I was traveling and broke. I had about five dollars, but I wasn't offering that information up. He asked me where I had been, where I was going, and why I was traveling.

"I've been all over the country. I've seen all sorts of things, including crossing the Mississippi River twice and going up and over the Continental Divide."

"That sounds really cool. Listen, if I buy you lunch, would you be interested in telling me about your trip?"

"Burger and coffee?" I asked.

"Sure. Anything you want."

"Then I hope you've got an hour."

We walked into the Burger King that adjoined the

station. He bought lunch and I told him about my travels.

"You should write a book," he told me.

"If I do, I'll tell everyone it was your idea," I joked. "At least I'll tell them you bought me lunch."

We finished our lunch and he looked at his watch, telling me he had to run or he'd miss his bus.

"Thanks for lunch,"

"You're welcome," he said as he ran off.

My bus wouldn't leave for another hour. I still had my notebook, so I looked at it. My note taking ability was pretty sad. I would be stuck in Philadelphia overnight on a long layover, so maybe I could pull my thoughts together with a cup of coffee and a light snack. It would keep me busy while I was waiting. It either that or I could take a nap.

CHAPTER SIXTEEN

The ride to Philadelphia was uneventful. Once again, there was a lack of people who wanted to talk. Maybe it was the area, or maybe my timing was just off. It was late when the bus got to Philadelphia, so there wasn't much of the city to see. When I got off the bus, the air was slightly chilly and the diesel fumes were particularly strong. The waiting area here was secured, unlike some stations, which means you had to show your ticket to get in.

The first thing I did was use the restroom. All of this traveling and I still hated the claustrophobic toilet on the bus. It was better than nothing in an emergency, but I avoided it if possible.

Being that it was so late, the coffee shop in the station was closed. I checked out the vending machine, but I realized that all I had left was a five dollar bill. That wasn't going to do me any good. I tried to remember if I had seen an all night restaurant, like a Howard Johnson's or a Denny's on the way in. I didn't remember seeing either one of those, but I did recall a diner that looked like it was within walking distance from where I was. I tried asking the security guard, but he wasn't terribly helpful. I decided to go on my own instincts. So I went out the door and headed up the street.

I hadn't got very far when I heard this voice. It wasn't like the voice in San Francisco, where I wasn't sure who it belonged to or where it was coming from. I could see exactly who it belonged to. There, under the street light, stood a short woman dressed in slacks and a satin jacket. She had a headful of curly hair with a lady's flat cap on her head. She leaned against the door of her car and called to me again.

"Son, where do you think you are going?"

"Who, me?" I asked, pointing at myself.

She pursed her lips and shook her head, "Of course you. Who else would I be speaking to here in the middle of the night? Now, just where do you think you are going?"

"To go get myself a cup of coffee. I thought I saw a diner down this way a few blocks. I figured I'd get a coffee to go and bring it back here."

"Oh no, you're not," talking to me like my

mother.

"I'm not?"

"No, you are not."

I was intrigued by the conversation with this woman to say the least. I walked closer to her, so I wouldn't be hollering across the road. As I got a better look at her, she reminded me of Shirley from the TV show *What's Happening*, just a little older.

"What should I be doing then?" I asked her politely.

"What you should be doing is going back inside and finding a spot to park your little white behind until your bus arrives. What you shouldn't be doing is wandering the streets at night. It's not exactly safe."

"I should be all right. I've been out at night before. I'll stay in the street lights."

"You're not listening to me," she said. "I'm telling you there are some boys around here who would like nothing more than to separate you from your money and give you a little common sense upside your head."

"Okay…" I said, starting to grasp her message.

"Also, if you have it in your head that you need coffee that badly, you can pay me to take you in my cab and I will walk you in."

"Seriously?"

"You seem like a nice boy. Not too bright, but nice. Now, I'm telling you to get back inside and sit down."

"All right, I will. Who are you, though, and why are you out here?"

"I'm a hack."

"I don't think you're that bad. You seem pretty nice to me."

She got a puzzled look on her face and looked me up and down. She started shaking her head.

"My word, they would have had fun with you."

"What do you mean?"

"I mean you're not from around here. That's obvious. I drive my own cab."

"Oh, so that's why you don't have a sign on

your car."

"Now you're catching on."

"So why do you do this?"

"Look at me. I gotta eat, and I ain't exactly gonna be a dancer."

"You're not that bad," I told her.

"You're nice and maybe a little blind. Maybe when you get home, you should get those eyes of yours checked out."

"Maybe."

"Now, listen," she said to me, "are you going to go inside or not? I've got to go to the airport to see if I can make some fares, because I'm not making anything talking to you.'

"You've convinced me. I'll go back inside. Thank you for looking out for me."

"You're welcome. I got boys of my own that ain't any smarter than you. Hopefully, someone is keeping an eye out for them."

"I hope so."

She climbed back in her car and watched as I

walked back inside. I turned and waved to her as she drove off.

"Good night!" I hollered at her car.

I opened the door of the station and went inside. After showing the security guy my ticket, I found a vacant seat, put my bag on my lap, and tipped my head forward. I soon heard a rush of people as I was waking up. I wasn't sure how long I had slept, so I sprung up to check the time. The bus I wanted was leaving now. I wasn't sure why I woke up when I did, but I was glad it happened. I was heading that much closer to home.

The next stop would be Scranton, and after that, Binghamton. The ride from Philadelphia to Scranton was scenic. That part of the country is as pretty as any, though sometimes you have to look a little harder. I had never got homesick before while traveling, but I might have had a touch of it now. The semi-familiar terrain of the northeast was nice to see.

The bus stopped in Scranton, and I spent most of my last five on something to eat. I hadn't eaten since Washington, D.C., and I was pretty hungry. After my meal, I had a dime, a penny and a toilet token in my pocket. My bus pass expired the day before, and I was the driver didn't notice, like the drive in Philadelphia.

When it came time to board, I was in luck. The driver looked at me, then looked at the ticket. He said, "Where're you heading?"

"Home."

"Good idea. Have a pleasant ride with us today." he said, waving me on, as if to let me know that he knew my ticket was no good.

"Thank you, sir. I will."

I walked to the middle of the bus and sat. Binghamton wasn't far away, and I'd need to change busses at least once more if I could just get away with it.

This ride went by really quick, and the names of places I'd heard of went by one after the other. I was in the final stretch and I knew it. The next sign said "Welcome to Binghamton, New York."

When I got off the bus, I checked the schedule. The bus I wanted was leaving now or sooner. I ran over to the bus and flashed my pass.

"Not so fast. Let me see that."

I handed him my Ameripass, and he looked at

it carefully. Then, he looked at me. I was hoping it would be the same result as in Scranton.

"Do you know this expired yesterday?"

"No, sir," I lied.

"Well, I'm afraid you'll have to buy another ticket to board this bus. You'll want to do it soon, because I'm leaving in a few minutes."

"Thank you, but I guess you'll be leaving without me."

I walked back inside, feeling a little dejected. I was glad to have made it this far, but now I had to figure out what I was going to do to get home. I walked outside and looked at the sky. It was going to rain. I had learned a valuable lesson about hitch-hiking in the rain: don't do it. I decided to call home and dialed collect.

"Hi, Mom. How are you?"

"I'm good. Are you okay? Where are you?"

"Yeah Ma, I'm fine. I have a question to ask. I'm stuck in Binghamton at the bus station. My pass expired and I'm broke. Do you think Dad could come and get me?"

Without hesitation, she replied, "Yes, he'll be there. Just stay put until he can get you."

"Thanks. I'll see you in a little while then."

"Bye. See you soon, honey."

With that, I hung up the phone and proceeded to walk around the bus station, examining the old woodwork and marble. I sat, stood, and waited impatiently, like a kid at school who couldn't wait for vacation.

Finally, several hours later, my dad walked in.

"Ready to go home?" he asked.

"I'm ready to sleep in my own bed."

The drive home went by quickly, with my dad and I discussing my trip. When we got to the house, I gave my mom a long hug and the souvenir mask I from New Orleans. I was pleased it was still in one piece. My mom was pleased I was still in one piece. We talked for a while, and I excused myself to take a shower and a nap.

Mark D. Webster

CHAPTER SEVENTEEN

After I had been home a few days and recharged my batteries, I started going out and looking up my friends. Some thought I was gone forever, because I left town so abruptly. Finally, one of my old friends caught up with me to tell me about the girl I had been seeing. She was dating another friend of ours, but I didn't care.

"What do you really think?" he asked me.

"I told you, I don't care. Now they can be each other's problem."

I started working at my old job shortly there after. I came home a different person. I had seen things and done things that my friends hadn't. It gave me a better perspective on the world, life, and myself. Now, almost thirty years later, I've learned that everything you do in life crafts you into something more than anyone can see. I know I couldn't travel that way again - my body and my wife wouldn't allow it - but what a great time I had following in the footsteps of my literary heroes. We should all be that lucky.

Mark D. Webster

Special Thanks to Justin Piatt for his great artwork. He does an amazing job taking my notions and running with them. I can't wait to work with him again!

NOTE FROM THE AUTHOR

When I first planned this book, it was going to be a work of fiction based on my actual trip. The problem was that I couldn't make up a story that was any more interesting than what actually happened. So, I decided to write the true story rather than make something up. Over time many of the pictures I took were lost, but a few still survived, thirty years later. Everything written here did happen, and the conversations were reconstructed to the best of my memory. I met a lot of interesting people and saw some wonderful things. I left most of the first names the same and only changed a few minor details when necessary. I hope you enjoy the story of my travels.

Mark D. Webster

Made in the USA
Middletown, DE
21 May 2015